Mysterious Monsters

Fact or Fiction?

Terry O'Neill, *Book Editor*

Daniel Leone, *President*

Bonnie Szumski, *Publisher*

Scott Barbour, *Managing Editor*

OPPOSING
VIEWPOINTS®
SERIES

GREENHAVEN
PRESS®

THOMSON
™
GALE

San Diego • Detroit • New York • San Francisco • Cleveland
New Haven, Conn. • Waterville, Maine • London • Munich

For more information, contact
Greenhaven Press
27500 Drake Rd.
Farmington Hills, MI 48331-3535
Or you can visit our Internet site at http://www.gale.com

Cover credit: © John Sibbick and Fortean Times/Fortean Picture Library

LIBRARY OF CONGRESS CATALOGING-IN-PUBLICATION DATA

Mysterious monsters / Terry O'Neill, book editor.
    p. cm. — (Fact or fiction?)
    Includes bibliographical references and index.
    ISBN 0-7377-1642-8 (pbk. : alk. paper) — ISBN 0-7377-1641-X (lib. : alk. paper)
        1. Monsters. I. O'Neill, Terry, 1944– . II. Fact or fiction? (Greenhaven Press)
    QL89.M98   2004
    001.944—dc21   2003049021

Printed in the United States of America

Contents

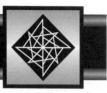

Foreword

"There are more things in heaven and earth, Horatio, than are dreamt of in your philosophy."
—William Shakespeare, *Hamlet*

"Extraordinary claims require extraordinary evidence."
—Carl Sagan, *The Demon-Haunted World*

Almost every one of us has experienced something that we thought seemed mysterious and unexplainable. For example, have you ever known that someone was going to call you just before the phone rang? Or perhaps you have had a dream about something that later came true. Some people think these occurrences are signs of the paranormal. Others explain them as merely coincidence.

As the examples above show, mysteries of the paranormal ("beyond the normal") are common. For example, most towns have at least one place where inhabitants believe ghosts live. People report seeing strange lights in the sky that they believe are the spaceships of visitors from other planets. And scientists have been working for decades to discover the truth about sightings of mysterious creatures like Bigfoot and the Loch Ness monster.

There are also mysteries of magic and miracles. The two often share a connection. Many forms of magical belief are tied to religious belief. For example, many of the rituals and beliefs of the voodoo religion are viewed by outsiders as magical practices. These include such things as the alleged Haitian voodoo practice of turning people into zombies (the walking dead).

There are mysteries of history—events and places that have been recorded in history but that we still have questions about today. For example, was the great King Arthur a real king or merely a legend? How, exactly, were the pyramids built? Historians continue to seek the answers to these questions.

Then, of course, there are mysteries of science. One such mystery is how humanity began. Although most scientists agree that it was through the long, slow process of evolution, not all scientists agree that indisputable proof has been found.

Subjects like these are fascinating, in part because we do not know the whole truth about them. They are mysteries. And they are controversial—people hold very strong and opposing views about them.

How we go about sifting through information on such topics is the subject of every book in the Greenhaven Press series Fact or Fiction? Each anthology includes articles that present the main ideas favoring and challenging a given topic. The editor collects such material from a variety of sources, including scientific research, eyewitness accounts, and government reports. In addition, a final chapter gives readers tools to analyze the articles they read. With these tools, readers can sift through the information presented in the articles by applying the methods of hypothetical reasoning. Examining these topics in this way adds a unique aspect to the Fact or Fiction? series. Hypothetical reasoning can be applied to any topic to allow a reader to become more analytical about the material he or she encounters. While such reasoning may not solve the mystery of who is right or who is wrong, it can help the reader separate valid from invalid evidence relating to all topics and can be especially helpful in analyzing material where people disagree.

The Search for Mysterious Monsters

The Witch-Cat

The tiny beast crouches and peers out from a tree in the night-time jungle, its huge pale eyes glowing in the moonlight. Its black fur makes it almost invisible in the darkness, but those who have seen it say that the third finger on each hand is strangely long and thin, and its ears are disproportionately large. Locals sometimes call this little goblin the witch-cat. They think its appearance foretells death, and they take care to avoid or kill it.[1]

The Loveland Frog

"On 3 March 1972, an anonymous police officer was driving on Riverside Road [in Loveland, Ohio], when he saw what looked like a dog on the icy road. He pulled over and shone his headlights on it. It suddenly stood up, jumped over the guardrail, and went down the embankment into the Miami River. The officer described the creature as being 3–4 feet tall, about 50–75 pounds, with leathery skin, and a frog or lizard-like face."[2] Two weeks later, another officer also reported seeing the creature.

Someone encountering creatures such as those described above would probably think they were frightening and mysterious monsters. Yet there are differences between the two. The witch-cat is actually an aye-aye, a member of the lemur family. It is actually shy and harmless. The strangest thing about it is that it had long been thought to be extinct; then, in 1986, three aye-ayes were discovered and captured by scientists for study. The second creature described above is not well documented. Most scientists consider it a myth or, at best, a misperception of a common animal—perhaps a dog, as the officer first thought he was seeing. Just as the aye-aye and the Loveland frog are quite different creatures, so are the people who study them. Scientists who study animals are called zoologists. However, there is a special field for people who study unknown animals—it is called cryptozoology, meaning "the study of hidden or unknown animals." The term was coined by French zoologist Bernard Heuvelmans in the 1950s. He is generally considered the father of cryptozoology because he was one of the first scientists to seriously consider mystery creatures.

Cryptozoologist Loren Coleman further defines cryptozoology as "the study of hidden animals . . . [that are at this time] not formally recognized by what is often termed Western science or zoology but [that are] supported in some way by testimony . . . from a human being."[3] Matthew Bille, another cryptozoologist, gave his first book a title that perfectly sums up the subject matter of cryptozoology: *Rumors of Existence: Newly Discovered, Supposedly Extinct, and Unconfirmed Inhabitants of the Animal Kingdom.* In very basic terms, zoologists try to learn all they can about known animals, and cryptozoologists seek knowledge about rumored animals—animals that have not yet been discovered, animals that are supposedly extinct—such as the aye-aye—but may not be, and legendary animals whose existence is unconfirmed. If there is a mysterious monster to be studied, it is likely that those who investigate it will be cryptozoologists.

The Living Fossil

In 1938 fishermen off the coast of South Africa hauled in the strangest catch of their life. It was five feet long and had stumpy, feetlike pectoral fins. The monster fish looked like nothing they had ever seen. In fact, when they took it ashore, it was so unusual that scientists studied it. They determined that it was a fish that had never before been seen by modern humans. The only prior evidence of its existence was in fossils millions of years old.[4]

The Mongolian Death Worm

"If you intrude upon the Allghoi khorkhoi, you risk death,"[5] say the people of Mongolia's remote Gobi Desert. People describe the Allghoi khorkhoi, or Mongolian death worm, as a fat, sausagelike worm that lives under the desert sands most of the year but emerges during the hot months of June and July. No one is quite sure how it kills its victims, but many think it is through spitting some kind of poison. It is said to have killed more than one hundred people during the twentieth century.

Deep-Sea Monster

"A ghostly, 23-foot-long creature glides through the deep sea, its gossamer fins billowing against the black water. Its arms, more than half its total length, trail behind like delicate threads,"[6] reported *Science* magazine in December 2002. Scientists said it is a species of squid so unusual that it is distinctly different from other known squids. Never before seen until very recently, squids like this one have been captured on videotape eight times in four different oceans.

Giant Ocean Worms

In 1977 scientists decended to the depths of the ocean off the Galapagos Islands to study continental drift. Author Matthew Bille reports, "Almost nine thousand feet down, [the] crew stared at a landscape from a science fiction film. Geothermal vents gushed hot, mineral-laden blue water from the ocean floor. Surrounding the vents was a densely packed colony of animals, many of which existed nowhere else. Tube worms, looking like eight-foot-long white hoses with red feather dusters poking from their open ends clustered at the site. . . . The animals had no mouths or digestive tract, just a section of brown, spongy tissue."[7]

Cryptozoology and the Search for Mysterious Monsters

Cryptozoology is not quite as well defined and established a science as zoology. A zoologist has an academic zoology degree, but cryptozoologists have various kinds of backgrounds. Some, like Heuvelmans and British cryptozoologist Karl P.N. Shuker, have zoology degrees. Others have scientific training in other fields, have training in investigation techniques, or are avid enthusiasts self-educated in cryptozoology. Although professional cryptozoologists such as Heuvelmans (deceased in 2001) and Shuker work hard to keep the profession on a sound scientific footing, many scientists do not consider it a serious field. This is not only because of the varied academic credentials (or lack of them) of the people who call themselves cryptozoologists, but also because of the strange subjects the field covers and because many of the "unknown" animals cryptozoologists study have little scientific evidence to support their existence. In essence, many cryptids (mystery animals) are little more than rumors to mainstream scientists.

What are some of the mysterious monsters cryptozoologists (and others) seek? Perhaps the best known are Bigfoot (also known as Sasquatch and by other names in other countries) and the Loch Ness monster. These two have captured and held the public imagination for decades. Others include the *chupacabras*, Mothman, the Dover Demon (all discussed in this book), the thunderbird, the Jersey Devil, and many more.

The nature of mysterious monsters makes them difficult to study scientifically. All are elusive—despite decades of hunting for them, no one has ever captured any of these creatures in the flesh. Few of them leave concrete physical evidence behind—evidence such as hair, fingerprints, teeth, or blood. In a few cases, bits of physical evidence have been found, but when they have been examined in scientific laboratories, the results have tended to be either negative or inconclusive. Bigfoot is one cryptid that has supposedly left footprints in a number of locations, but the results of analysis of those footprints have been debated for many years. Some are clearly fakes, and scientists, including zoologists and cryptozoologists, cannot reach agreement on whether others are genuine evidence of a mysterious monster. Likewise, photographs and even movie film have been taken of some cryptids, but, again, analysis is inconclusive. The pictures tend to be taken from a distance, resulting in fuzzy pictures so that it is almost impossible to tell what they actually show.

What this means is that the strongest evidence of mysterious monsters tends to be anecdotal. Robert T. Carroll, who operates the Skeptic's Dictionary website (www.skepdic. com), says cryptozoology "relies heavily upon testimonials and circumstantial evidence in the form of legends and folklore, and the stories and alleged sightings of mysterious beasts by indigenous peoples, explorers, and travelers."[8] For example, the people of Tibet have reported encounters with the Yeti (similar to the Bigfoot of North America) for centuries. Many of these reports are highly detailed, describing the creature's appearance, smell, and sounds, and have been given by people deemed reliable. Yet many scientists say this is not enough. They ask, if the Yeti exists, why has no one ever captured one? Wildlife Conservation Society biologist Kent Redford responds, "What a bankrupt world it would be if you refused to believe things existed until you actually had seen a specimen in a museum. I mean, there are lots of things we are prepared to believe exist without having seen them."[9] He points to subatomic particles as one example. However, a significant difference between cryptozoological creatures and subatomic particles is that scientists have been able to perform certain kinds of experiments that provide more solid evidence of the existence of subatomic particles than anyone has been able to provide so far for the Yeti or any other mysterious monster.

Ben S. Roesch, editor of the *Cryptozoology Review* and host of an informative cryptozoology website (www.ncf.carleton. ca/~bz2050/HomePage.cryptoz.html), says that some of the criticism leveled against cryptozoology is justified:

> In many cases, cryptozoologists are too carefree in their con-clusions and don't bother to incorporate scientific data that refutes what they are proposing. Occam's razor [a theory that says the simplest explanation is often the best] is gen-erally not applied with sufficient rigour—I often find that many cryptozoological theories can be explained equally well with alternatives that are less radical and more consis-tent with accepted facts.[10]

In other words, looking at the Loveland frog anecdote above, a dog is a simpler explanation than a bizarre, giant frog-creature. If the known facts fit a dog at least as well as they fit a mysterious monster, using Occam's razor, a per-son would probably conclude that what the officers saw was a dog.

Still, there are cryptozoologists who pursue their quarry with scientific rigor to the degree that they are able. They use statistical analysis of witness reports and laboratory analysis of what meager evidence they find, in addition to thor-oughly examining witnesses and their stories. And they con-tinue to believe that one day they will find conclusive evi-dence of a mysterious monster that lurks in the wilderness.

Amazon Monster

"'I was working by the river when I heard a scream, a horri-ble scream,' the now 70-year-old [hunter João Batista] Azevedo told Reuters [news agency] by telephone from his remote Amazon village. 'Suddenly something looking like a man came out of the forest all covered with fur. He was walking on two legs and thank God he did not come toward us.'" Others have described this creature as about six feet tall, built extremely powerfully, "capable of breaking thick roots with his footsteps," and emitting a terrible smell, "a mixture of feces and rotting flesh."[11]

Giant Bird

"He's huge, he's huge, he's really, really big." So said pilot John Bouker about the gigantic bird the size of a small airplane that he and several others reported seeing fly over southwest Alaska in October 2002. According to the *Anchorage Daily News* on October 15 that year, Bouker had been skeptical when he had heard other reports of giant birds. Then he and his airline passengers saw it for themselves.[12]

Winged Cats

In 1995 in Cumbria, England, tourist Martin Milner encountered a large, friendly tabby cat "with a very distinctive pair of fluffy wings," reports zoologist and cryptozoologist Karl P.N. Shuker. And in the 1970s photos were taken of a cat mascot at a Manchester, England, construction firm. The cat had furry wings "sprouting from its shoulders, each . . . measuring 11 inches, thereby yielding an impressive 22-inch wingspan."[13]

Monkey Man

In May 2001, citizens of New Delhi, India, and nearby towns were terrorized by a mysterious apelike creature that had the head of a monkey and the body of a man. The creature leaped from roof to roof and pounced on people, biting and scratching them. The police distributed portraits of the creature to its officers with orders to shoot on sight.[14]

The Fascination with Monsters

When questioning the existence of mysterious monsters, one of the most puzzling aspects is the number of people who say they have encountered them—seen them, heard them, smelled them, been threatened by them, or seen the results of their sometimes savage activities. As author John

Keel writes, "No matter where you live on this planet, someone within two hundred miles of your home has had a di-
rect confrontation with a frightening apparition or inexplicable 'monster.' . . . An almost infinite variety of known and
unknown creatures thrive on this mudball [Earth] and appear regularly year after year, century after century."[15] How
can thousands of reports be explained if not by the existence of mysterious monsters the witnesses think they have
encountered?

In the more straightforward cases, "mysterious monsters"
are easily explained by hoaxes and misperceptions of more
ordinary things. (For example, in the Loveland frog anecdote above, the officers may have misperceived a dog and
only thought they saw a monster.) However, there are other
explanations to consider as well. People have reported
monsters as long as humanity has existed, and even more
people who have not encountered monsters themselves believe in them. If such creatures do not exist, why do people
continue to report and believe in them? Some psychologists
say that people *need* monsters. In ancient myths, monsters
were often used as the explanation for why bad things happen to good people. For people today, monsters can provide
cautionary lessons, help one deal with one's own dark side,
and provide pleasurably fearful mental stimulation.

Cautionary lessons. Sometimes a myth or legend about a
monster can teach or reinforce an important lesson. For example, geographer Nigel Smith thinks that native people's
stories about the Amazon monster described above provide
an important ecological safeguard. The monster is said to
travel with white-lipped peccaries (wild pigs), protecting
these porcine herds and wreaking terrible revenge on any
overzealous hunter it catches. Smith says that such stories
ensure that the people of the jungle do not deplete their
natural resources (such as the peccary). Similarly, when

adults tell children tales of the boogieman—or the Bigfoot or *chupacabras*—lurking in the nearby woods, such tales help protect uncautious children from harm by discouraging them from venturing into environments they are not prepared to handle.

Dealing with the dark side. Some people believe that consideration of monsters can help people explore their own dark side. "The monster is the alien in our minds," says Italian criminologist Francesco Sidoti. "He's the inexplicable, the incredible, and the inadmissible that has finally become visible and tangible. The radical otherness of the monster can help us define ourselves."[16] By confronting a monster, whether in real life or vicariously through the experiences of others, people are made to examine their own characters. How is the monster different from themselves? Or, more frightening, how is it alike? How would they behave if they met such a creature? By thinking about and answering such questions, people can develop a better understanding of their own characters.

Mental stimulation. Patrick Macias, the author of *Tokyo-Scope: The Japanese Cult Film Companion*, says that monsters provide much-needed mental exercise: "The human imagination needs exercise to stay healthy, and grappling with the weird and horrible offers a major mental workout."[17] Andrew Greeley, a Catholic priest and novelist (now deceased), would probably concur. In an interview about why people are attracted to vampires, he said that such creatures fulfill "a hunger for the marvelous." Especially in today's world, where many people have lapsed from traditional spiritual beliefs, when they have "given up angels and devils," he says, "some people are going to turn to aliens, Darth Vader [a character from the *Star Wars* movies], and vampires. Life seems to be dull and unexciting, . . . so you have to hunt for something marvelous enough to bring back the excitement."[18]

Tantalizing Mysteries

Certainly, excitement is one reason cryptozoologists search for mysterious monsters and one reason people continue to believe in them. For what could be more exciting than at last discovering irrefutable evidence of a creature that so many people refuse to believe in. The thrill of the unknown, a search for explanations, an answer to a mystery—all of these keep cryptozoologists and others on the trail of mysterious monsters.

Notes

1. The witch-cat is the aye-aye, a nocturnal, insect-eating member of the lemur family. It is native to Madagascar and until recently was thought to be extinct. In 1986 two adults and a juvenile were captured. Presently, only a small number of aye-ayes exist in the wild. *Accepted by science.*

2. Davy Russell, "The Loveland Frog." www.xproject.net/archives/cryptozoology/lovelandfrog.html. *Not accepted by science.*

3. Loren Coleman, "The Meaning of Cryptozoology." www.ncf.carleton.ca/~bz050/HomePage.czmean.html.

4. The monster fish was a coelacanth. According to cryptozoologist Matthew Bille, "The coelacanth is a survivor of the lobe-finned fishes, which, it is believed, gave rise to the amphibians, which in turn evolved into the reptiles, mammals, and birds." Until the 1938 catch, the coelacanth was thought to have died out millions of years ago. Matthew Bille, *Rumors of Existence: Newly Discovered, Supposedly Extinct, and Unconfirmed Inhabitants of the Animal Kingdom.* Blaine, WA: Hancock House, 1995, p. 25. *Accepted by science.*

5. Ivan Makerle, "In Search of the Killer Worm," *Fate,* June 1996. *Not accepted by science:* Most scientists think that if an unknown, dangerous desert "worm" exists, it is probably a misperceived more common creature, such as a snake or lizard.

6. Kathleen Wren, "Giant Squid Is Something 'Fundamentally Different,' Illustrating How Little We Know About the Ocean's Depths," *Science,* December 2002. Go to www.msnbc.com/news/674647.asp to see a brief video clip of this amazing monster. *Accepted by science.*

7. Bille, *Rumors of Existence,* pp. 36–37. *Accepted by science.*

8. Robert T. Carroll, "Cryptozoology," the Skeptic's Dictionary. http://skepdic.com/crypto.html.

9. Quoted in Marguerite Holloway, "Beasts in the Mist," *Discover,* September 1999, p. 62.

10. Ben S. Roesch, "On the Nature of Cryptozoology and Science," ForteanTimes. com. http://217.206.205.125/exclusive/cryptoscience.shtml.

11. This monster is called a *mapinguari* by the Brazilian Indians. It is thought to emit its horrid stench as a kind of defensive mechanism. David Oren, an ornithologist and expert on Amazonian biodiversity, thinks it is a giant ground sloth, believed by most scientists to be long extinct. Creature Chronicles.

http://home.fuse.net/rschaffner/wildlife.html. *Not accepted by most scientists.*

12. Reported in various newspapers. *Scientists still are not sure what Bouker and others observed.*

13. Karl P.N. Shuker, "Wonderful Things Are Cats with Wings," *Fate*, April 1996, p. 80. Several such cats have been documented. They suffer from a condition called feline cutaneous asthenia, which gives them "abnormally elastic skin that stretches at the slightest touch," according to cryptozoologist Shuker. Sometimes the "wings" contain muscle fiber that allows the cat to move them; often the "wings" are so fragile that they fall off easily with no bleeding. *Accepted by scientists.*

14. Reported in various newspapers. Since panicked citizens' descriptions of the mystery creature varied significantly, experts conjecture that rather than being a human-ape beast, the attacker is one or more of the wild monkeys that occasionally attack people for no reason. *Not accepted by scientists.*

15. John Keel, *The Complete Guide to Mysterious Beings*, rev. ed. New York: Doubleday, 1994, pp. 1–2.

16. Francesco Sidoti, "Are Human Rights for Monsters, Too?" *Mediterranean Journal of Human Rights*, 1999, p. 467.

17. Patrick Macias, "Where Is King Kong When We Need Him?" *Salon.* www.salon.com/media/media960725.html.

18. Quoted in Katherine Ramsland, "Hunger for the Marvelous: The Vampire Craze in the Computer Age," *Vampire Junction.* www.afn.org/~vampires/psychology.html.

Chapter 1

Fact or Fiction?

Mysterious
Monsters Exist

We Saw Mothman

Linda Scarberry

In late 1966, people in the little town of Point Pleasant, West Virginia, and the surrounding area began seeing strange things in the sky. Over a period of only a few weeks, hundreds of people reported seeing UFOs. Then on the night of November 15, two young married couples were joyriding near an abandoned munitions plant, called the TNT area, outside of town. They saw something that night they would never forget: a huge, humanlike figure with wings and glowing red eyes. At first thrilled, then terrified, they soon drove back to town and called the police.

Over the next few weeks, several more people saw the creature, which came to be known as Mothman. The creature received nationwide publicity when a freelance reporter, John Keel, wrote a series of newspaper articles and a book called *The Mothman Prophecies*.

Mothman disappeared just as quickly as he appeared. After about three unforgettable weeks, he seemed to have left Point Pleasant. Sporadic Mothman sightings have been reported over the years in Point Pleasant and elsewhere, as have sightings of similar creatures, but never again in such numbers.

Mothman has intrigued people for many years, and in 2000, two young men from Point Pleasant—Donnie Sergent Jr. and Jeff Wamsley—compiled a book of documents about the 1966 events. The following eyewitness account is taken from that book. It was written by Linda Scarberry, one of the original eyewitnesses, a few days after she and her friends saw Mothman. At the time Sergent and Wamsley compiled the book, Scarberry's companions did not want to once again be involved in the weird notoriety surrounding Mothman, so they are identified simply as Eyewitnesses #1, #2, and #3.

We were riding through the TNT Area on a side road by the old Power house building around 12:00 on Tuesday night Nov. 15th, 1966 when we came over this small rise in the road. All at once [Eyewitness #3] yelled for us to look at that thing in the road. I looked up and saw it go around the corner at the old Power House. It didn't run but wobbled like it couldn't keep its balance. Its wings were spread just a little. We sat there a few seconds then [Eyewitness #2] took off. I kept yelling for him to hurry. We didn't even stop for the curves. We got out on Route 62 and was coming down the road and that thing was sitting on the second hill when you come into the 1st bad curves. As soon as our lights hit it, it was gone. It spread its wings a little and went straight up into the air.

When we got to the armory it was flying over our car. We were going between 100 and 105 mph down that straight stretch and that thing was just gliding back and forth over the back end of the car. As we got there in front of the lights by the Resort it dived at our car and went away. I could hear the wings flapping as if to get more speed as it went up. We were all terrified and kept yelling for [Eyewitness #2] to go faster. As we came into that straight stretch by C.C. Lewis' [farm] the thing was over our car again. Then it disappeared as we came into the lights by C.C. Lewis' gates. We went on downtown and stopped at Dairyland and tried to decide what to do. We just sat there and looked at each other.

A Dead Dog and a Winged Monster

I wanted to go to the police but [Eyewitness #3] and [Eyewitness #2] kept saying they'd just laugh at us. We talked about it awhile and [Eyewitness #2] and [Eyewitness #3] wanted to go back up the road. [Eyewitness # 1] and I kept trying to talk them out of it and finally when we got to C.C. Lewis' gate they decided they didn't want to go back up so we turned around. As we were turning we saw a big dead dog laying along the road. When we were almost turned around this thing jumped out from behind something and leaped over our car and went through the field on the other side of the road. We decided to go to the police then and went down and around Tiny's Drive-In looking for them. [Eyewitness #4] was outside the Drive Inn getting ready to take a couple boys home so we told him about seeing this thing and asked him to call the police. After the police came we went back up the road in our car with [Eyewitness #4] and the police about ½ mile behind us. I saw it then in a pasture field with its wings out a little walking towards the car then it went up in the air and came at the car.

As [Eyewitness #4]'s car lights came over the rise in the road and the lights shined on it, it disappeared. We went up and down the road looking for it but didn't see anymore. We went back down to the drive in and got in [Eyewitness #4]'s car and went back up. We finally found [Eyewitness

#5] and got with him and went to the powerhouse building. We sat there with our lights out for about 15 or 20 minutes when I heard that squeaking sound like a mouse only a lot stronger. A shadow went across the building and the dogs started barking over on the hill across from us. [Eyewitness # 1] and I saw the red eyes then and told [Eyewitness #5]. He shined the lights right on them without being told where they were. We saw dust coming from the ground or somewhere as [Eyewitness #5] moved the spotlight around. We finally left and came to the trailer. [Two of them] were afraid to go to their apartment so we decided to stay together but we didn't go to bed. We just turned on all the lights and stayed up.

Exploring the Scene

Wednesday we went up again to the building and found these odd tracks around the building. [Eyewitness #3] was around the boilers by himself and suddenly he came running out white as a sheet yelling for someone. He said he saw it in the boiler. That night it was seen at [Eyewitness #6]'s so we went up there and [Eyewitness #1] and I stayed in the house while [Eyewitness #3] and [Eyewitness #2] and a few others [bystanders] went looking for it. On the way up I saw it from the highway above the trees gliding back and forth. They searched the area around [Eyewitness #6]'s house but didn't find anything. We started home around 12:30 and I saw it in one of the maintenance buildings. [Eyewitness #1] and I started crying and [Eyewitness #2] took off. I kept thinking about that thing following us again but it didn't. We went to my mothers' and I went all to pieces. [Eyewitness #2] and my dad took me down to the hospital. I finally got back home and we all stayed together that night again but didn't go to bed till 3 or 4 o'clock. We were still afraid to go to sleep. The next day Thursday we went back up with reporters and we all heard a clanging noise from inside the building. [Eyewitness #2], [Eyewitness #3] and the reporters went back in and found the boiler door open that [Eyewitness #3] had shut when he left a few minutes before that. That night we went back up and Mary Hyre and I saw the eyes inside the fenced off place beside the Power house building. On the way home I saw its eyes back in some trees from the road as the car went past and looked back and could see its form. That is the last time I have seen it.

A Man with Wings

To me it just looks like a man with wings. [It was a dirty grey color.] It has a body shape form with wings on its back that come around it. It has muscular legs like a man and fiery-red eyes that glow when the lights hit it. There was no glowing about it until the lights hit it. I couldn't see its head or arms. I don't know if the eyes are even in a head. When we came down the straight stretch by the armory it didn't even seem like it had any trouble keeping up with us. It must have had very powerful wings. At no time did this thing fly at us from the front of the car. It stayed over the back end of the car while it was chasing us. It seemed to be afraid of lights but I read in the paper today that it has been seen in the day time in town. That I don't understand. The prints we found at C.C. Lewis' gate and at both Powerhouses and at [Eyewitness #6]'s. . . . They looked like 2 horse shoes put together but they're smooth.

I know people are laughing at us but it's no laughing matter. We'll never forget this thing. It has affected our lives in many ways. I am keeping going on nerve and sleeping pills. When it gets dark I feel the fear creeping over me. When I go anyplace I automatically look up and out the windows. I am afraid to sleep at night so I lay awake sometimes crying with fear. When I do sleep or go to bed the lights burn all night. Even in the daylight I'm afraid to be by myself. I walk around in my own house expecting to see that thing. I close my eyes day or night and I can see those red fiery eyes staring at me. Every little noise scares me to death. I can stand in a crowd and hear people talking about us and laughing. People have said we were probably "liquored up" but we were NOT. They go up there expecting to see it but then they say they don't believe us. We HAVE seen it so we know what to look for and we are constantly looking—not because we want to see it—but because we're afraid we'll see it again. Out of all the phone calls we've gotten not one minister has called to help us or try to explain what it is. We all agree we'd like to talk to a minister about it but no one takes us that serious. One minister even laughed and said they'd finally run the devil out of their church and that's what we saw. We've been harassed and laughed at and called crazy.

We just can't go up there and hand it to people on a silver platter like they seem to want us to do. We are never really going to get over our fear until we find out for sure what this thing is. I know I'll never forget it. I don't think anyone can who has seen it.

Mothman Is a Paranormal Creature

John A. Keel

John A. Keel was a freelance reporter in 1966. Long interested in the paranormal ("beyond the normal"), Keel was in the process of writing a book about UFOs when he heard about strange events happening in the little town of Point Pleasant, West Virginia. People in the area had been reporting hundreds of UFO sightings, and then several people reported seeing a frightening, manlike winged creature. They didn't know whether the creature was associated with the UFOs or not, but they were worried about what it was and what it was doing at Point Pleasant.

During his years studying UFOs and other unusual occurrences, Keel had noticed that paranormal events tended to follow a pattern—for example, a flurry of UFO reports would come from a certain area of the country, then abruptly stop. The same pattern was often true for sightings of strange creatures. Keel began to develop a theory connecting all of these events. He theorized that Mothman and other paranormal "winged men," who have been reported as long ago as the time of the ancient Greek philosopher Plato and up to today, exist in a separate dimension and spend much of their time manipulating humanity. The "winged men" include the Garudas from ancient India, fairies from many cultures, "sky serpents" seen in nineteenth-century America, the Owlman seen in England in the 1970s, and others. Sometimes the appearance of one of these entities brings a warning, sometimes merely fear or mystery. The title of one of Keel's books, *Disneyland of the Gods*, expresses his theory that people on Earth are part of the "Disneyland" with which these paranormal entities entertain themselves.

When Keel heard about the mysterious monster at Point Pleasant, he traveled there and interviewed more than a hundred people. He went to the sites where Mothman was seen, hoping to witness the monster for himself. He discovered that many elements of what some paranormal researchers call "high strangeness" seemed to be related to the Mothman sightings. These included visits to witnesses from mysterious strangers, some of whom purported to be from the government and who tried to discourage people from talking about Mothman; strange phone calls to Keel and to many of the Mothman witnesses that consisted of weird electronic tones or mysterious voices asking odd questions and predicting disasters, including one at Point Pleasant; poltergeist activity; and other bizarre occurrences.

Abruptly, after a few weeks, the Mothman sightings ceased. Then, a year later, the Silver Bridge, a forty-year-old bridge spanning the river between Gallipolis, Ohio, and Point Pleasant, collapsed, dropping thirty-seven cars and trucks into the frigid waters and killing forty-six people. Keel became convinced that, somehow, the Mothman sightings and the other weird occurrences had been harbingers of the bridge disaster. He wrote a book, *The Mothman Prophecies*, that details his experiences and those of the people at Point Pleasant (and discusses many other kinds of weirdness that seemed to support his theory about paranormal entities manipulating humankind). *The Mothman Prophecies* was adapted into a popular 2002 movie.

The following article is taken from another of Keel's books and tells about some of the strange occurrences in Point Pleasant during the time Mothman was a visitor.

Five men were digging a grave in a cemetery near Clendenin, West Virginia, on November 12, 1966, when something that looked like "a brown human being" fluttered from some nearby trees and maneuvered low over their heads. "It was gliding through the trees," witness Kenneth Duncan of Blue Creek said, "and was in sight for about a minute."

The men were baffled. It did not look like any kind of a bird but seemed to be a man with wings. They discussed it with a few friends and would have forgotten about it if others in West Virginia had not also started seeing the enigmatic flier.

About a year earlier, a woman living on the Ohio River, some miles from Clendenin, was amused when her seven-year-old son ran into the house one day and excitedly told her that he had seen "an angel . . . a man with wings." She assumed it was just his imagination and thought no more about it.

In the summer of 1966 another woman in the Ohio Valley, the wife of a doctor, was in her backyard when a six-foot-long thing soared past her very rapidly. She thought it resembled a "giant butterfly" and she dared to mention the incident to only a few people. But all of these random, anomalous events were only the prologue to the "monster mania" which would grip the whole western edge of West Virginia in November 1966.

A Mysterious Monster

[Another man,] Newell Partridge, had seen two glowing red objects in a field near Salem, West Virginia, on the night of November 14, 1966. His dog, Bandit, a German shepherd, had run into the field and vanished. The very next night around midnight, two young couples, Mr. and Mrs. Roger Scarberry and Mr. and Mrs. Steve Mallette, were driving through an abandoned World War II ammunition dump known as the TNT Area, seven miles outside of Point Pleasant, West Virginia, when, as they passed an old deserted power plant, they saw a weird figure standing beside the road staring at them.

"It was shaped like a man, but bigger," Roger Scarberry said later. "Maybe six and a half or seven feet tall. And it had big wings folded against its back."

"But it was those eyes that got us," Linda Scarberry declared with a shudder. "It had two big red eyes, like automobile reflectors."

"For a minute we could only stare at it," Roger continued. "Then it just turned and sort of shuffled towards the open door of the old power plant. We didn't wait around."

Roger stepped on the gas pedal of his souped-up jalopy and headed out of the TNT Area for Route 62 which leads into Point Pleasant. As they shot down the highway ("We were doing better than a hundred miles per hour," Roger claimed), his wife cried out, "It's following us!"

All four swore that the "Bird" was low overhead, its wings spread out to about ten feet. It seemed to keep up with the car effortlessly even though its wings were not flapping.

"I could hear it making a sound," Mrs. Mallette, an attractive eighteen-year-old brunette stated. "It squeaked . . . like a big mouse."

"It followed us right to the city limits," Roger went on. "Funny thing, we noticed a dead dog by the side of the road there, but when we came back a few minutes later, the dog was gone."

The panic-stricken quartet drove directly to the office of the Mason County sheriff and excitedly poured out their story to Deputy Millard Halstead.

"I've known them all their lives," Halstead told us during our first visit to Point Pleasant. "They've never been in any trouble. I took them seriously."

Deputy Halstead returned to the TNT Area with them. As he parked outside the abandoned power plant the police radio in his car suddenly emitted a strange sound like a speeded-up phonograph record. He shut the radio off. The "Bird," however, was nowhere to be found.

The next day a press conference was held in the County Courthouse and the four young people repeated their story. One of the reporters there, Mrs. Mary Hyre, Point Pleasant correspondent for the Athens, Ohio, *Messenger* and local stringer for the Associated Press, later told us, "I've heard them repeat their story a hundred times now to reporters from all over and none of them have ever changed it or added a word."

News of the Scarberry-Mallette sighting was flashed around the world. It even appeared in the Pacific edition of the [military newspaper] *Stars & Stripes*. Television camera crews from Huntington and Charleston invaded Point Pleasant, and that night the normally deserted TNT Area resembled Times Square on New Year's Eve. But Steve Mallette announced, "I've seen it once. I hope I never see it again.". . .

"Mothman" cut crazy capers all over West Virginia that November. Sightings were reported in Mason, Lincoln, Logan, Kanawha, and Nicholas Counties. Most of the population remained skeptical but the near-hysteria of the rapidly multiplying witnesses was very real. Police in the city of Charleston, West Virginia, received an excited phone call from one Richard West at 10:15 P.M., Monday, November 21. Patrolman D.L. Tucker handled the call. West insisted that a "Batman" was sitting on a roof next to his home. "It looks like a man. It's about six feet tall and has a wingspread of six or eight feet," West reported excitedly. "It has great big red eyes."

"Did it fly?" Tucker asked.

"Straight up, just like a helicopter," West answered.

In St. Albans, West Virginia, just outside of Charleston, Mrs. Ruth Foster claimed that "Mothman" appeared on her front lawn on the evening of November 26.

"It was standing on the lawn beside the porch," she told reporters. "It was tall, with big red eyes that popped out of its face. My husband is six feet one and the 'Bird' looked about the same height, or a little shorter, maybe.

"It had a funny little face. I didn't see any beak. All I saw were those big red poppy eyes. I screamed and ran back into the house. My brother-in-law went out to look, but it was gone."

The day before, on November 25, Thomas Ury was driving along Route 62 just north of the TNT Area. The time was 7:15 A.M. He noticed a tall, gray man-like figure standing in a field by the road. "Suddenly it spread a pair of wings," Ury said, "and took off straight up, like a helicopter.

"It veered over my convertible and began going in circles three telephone poles high," he continued. "It kept flying right over my car even though I was doing about seventy-five."

Mr. Ury rocketed into Point Pleasant and went straight to

Sheriff George Johnson. "I never saw anything like it," he confided to Mrs. Hyre later. "I was so scared I just couldn't go to work that day. This thing had a wingspan every bit of ten feet. It could be a bird, but I certainly never saw one like it. I was afraid it was going to come down right on top of me."

Terrifying Red Eyes

Miss Connie Carpenter, a shy, studious girl of eighteen from New Haven, West Virginia, had an identical encounter at 10:30 A.M., Sunday, November 27. She was driving home from church when she saw what she thought at first was a large man in gray standing on the deserted links of the Mason County Golf Course outside of Mason, West Virginia, on Route 62. Those ten-foot wings suddenly unfolded, the thing took off straight up and headed for her car.

"Those eyes! They were a very red and once they were fixed on me I couldn't take my own eyes off them," she declared. "It's a wonder I didn't have a wreck."

She said the creature flew directly at her windshield, then veered off and disappeared. Connie stepped on the gas and raced home in hysteria. She was so upset that she was unable to go to school for several days and required medical attention. She was the only "Mothman" witness to suffer from a common UFO ailment—*klieg conjunctivitus* or "eye-burn." Her eyes were red, swollen and itchy for two weeks afterwards. Many witnesses to low-flying UFOs suffer this same thing, apparently caused by actinic (ultra-violet) rays.

Miss Carpenter was also one of the few to claim a close look at the "Mothman's" face. "It was horrible . . . like something out of a science-fiction movie.". . .

Shortly after the first "Mothman" stories hit the local papers, a wide variety of explanations were expressed by assorted experts. Dr. Robert Smith of the West Virginia University Biology Department declared that everyone was obviously seeing a rare sandhill crane. A bird whose long neck and long legs can give it a height of six feet, and it has red patches around the eyes. Yet no hunter in the area has reported seeing such a crane, and members of the zoology department of Ohio University pointed out that the crane inhabits the plains of Canada and has never been seen in the West Virginia–Ohio region.

We carried photos of sandhill cranes and other birds (including the *Pterodactyl*) with us during our investigations in West Virginia. "That's not the thing we saw," Roger Scarberry scoffed when he saw the pictures. "This thing could never chase us like it did."

"I just wish Dr. Smith could see the thing," Mary Mallette added.

All those who reported having seen "Mothman" sneered at the crane theory, but the skeptics, and they were in the majority, quickly accepted it and dismissed the mystery. Three groups of witnesses contributed to the confusion by declaring that they were convinced that the "Bird" was really some kind of giant ornithological oddity and not a "monster from outer space" as some were beginning to imply. . . .

Weird Happenings

The McDaniel family [whose daughter, Linda Scarberry, was one of the original "Mothman" witnesses] had been living in the twilight zone ever since their daughter and the others had first glimpsed "Mothman." Linda had repeatedly heard the sound "of a speeded-up phonograph record" around her own home after the incident and peculiar manifestations indicating the presence of a poltergeist began. Finally she and Roger moved into the basement apartment in the McDaniel's home. The poltergeist followed them. Strange lights appeared in the house, objects moved by themselves, and the heavy odor of cigar smoke was frequently noted. No one in the family smokes. (The smell of cigar smoke is commonly reported in many poltergeist cases throughout the world.) One morning Linda woke up and distinctly saw the shadowy form of a large man in the room. The house was searched. All the doors were still locked. There was no sign of a prowler. . . .

Beginning in the fall of 1966 the TV sets and telephones in the region began to go wild, as strange blobs of crystaline white light appeared in the night skies. Many of these lights moved at tree-top level. There were also many daylight sightings of strange circular objects, *particularly in the TNT Area.* By the end of 1967 over one thousand UFO sightings by responsible witnesses had been recorded throughout the Valley. Cars passing along the Camp Conley Road, south of the TNT Area, stalled inexplicably. Television sets and radios, some brand new, burned out suddenly without cause. In March–April 1967 the UFO sightings hit an incredible peak with the objects appearing nightly at low level over the TNT Area as if they were following a regular flight schedule. Thousands of people invaded the section again to view this new wonder. Sheriff Johnson and most of his men were among the witnesses but soberly refused to comment on the phenomenon. . . .

Mrs. Hyre received a long line of very strange visitors after her UFO and "Mothman" stories began to appear in the press. Early in January 1967 she was working late in her office across from the County Court House when a little man entered. He was about four feet six inches tall, she said later, and had very strange eyes covered with thick-lensed glasses. His black hair was long and cut squarely "like a bowl haircut." Although it was about 20° F outside he was wearing a short-sleeved blue shirt and blue trousers of thin material. He kept his right hand in his pocket at all times.

Speaking in a low, halting voice, he asked her for directions to Welsh, West Virginia. She thought at first that he had some kind of speech impediment, and for some reason he terrified her. "He kept getting closer and closer," she said, "his funny eyes staring at me almost hypnotically."

Alarmed, she ran into the back room where the newspaper's circulation manager was working on a telephone campaign. He joined her and they spoke together to the little man. "He seemed to know more about West Virginia than we did," she declared.

At one point the telephone rang, and while she was speaking on it the little man picked up a ball-point pen from her desk and looked at it in amazement, "as if he had never seen a pen before." She gave him a pen and said he laughed in a loud, strange way as he took it. Then he ran out into the night and disappeared around a corner.

Being a good newspaperwoman, Mrs. Hyre later checked with the police to find out if there was any mentally deficient person on the loose who fitted the little man's description. There wasn't.

Several weeks later Mrs. Hyre was crossing the street near her office when she again saw this very same man. He appeared startled when he noticed her watching him, turned abruptly, and ran for a large black car which suddenly rounded the corner. It was driven by a very large man. The little man sprang into it and it sped away. . . .

At 5:05 P.M. on the evening of December 15, 1967, the seven-hundred-span linking Point Pleasant with Ohio suddenly collapsed laden with rush hour traffic, carrying forty-six vehicles into the dark waters of the Ohio River. That night the Lilly family on Camp Conley Road divided their attention between their TV set and the eerie lights that were racing at tree-top level over the woods behind their home. They counted twelve UFOs altogether, more than they had ever seen on a single evening before. No UFOs were reported in Point Pleasant proper on that tragic night. . . .

What the Eyewitnesses Reported

In the majority of all the "Mothman" cases, the witnesses managed only a brief glimpse of the creature. Its most outstanding feature seemed to be its glowing red eyes. Self-luminous eyes usually suggest a paraphysical entity rather than a real animal. About half of the witnesses appeared to be people with latent or active psychic abilities, prone to having accurate premonitions, prophetic dreams, extra-sensory perception (ESP), etc. Few witnesses were able to describe the "Bird's" face, but most noted the eyes and were admittedly terrified by them. The eyes seemed to have been more terrifying than the tremendous size of the creature. While some people claimed that "Mothman" was brown, most have described it as being grayish in color. All witnesses agreed that the wings did not flap in flight, making its incredible speeds all the more unaccountable. Those who saw it walk said that it shuffled or "waddled" penguin-like. Those who claimed to have seen it take off said it rose straight up like a helicopter.

Considering its reported size, the ten-foot wingspread does not make sense. A normal-sized man would require wings twenty to thirty feet wide in order to glide and support his weight. Most large birds must make a running start to get airborne.

The following composite description of West Virginia's "Mothman" has been compiled from more than one hundred eye-witness accounts:

1. HEIGHT: Between five and seven feet tall. Usually described as "taller than a goodsized man."
2. BREADTH: Broad at the top with slight taper downwards. Always described as "very broad, much broader than a man."
3. COVERING: Witnesses have been unable to determine if it is clothed or covered with skin. Generally

described as being gray, though some thought it was brown. One witness thought it was covered with gray fur. Daylight sightings of others do not substantiate this.

4. HEAD: Seen from the back it appears to have no head. Few witnesses reported seeing any face at all.

5. EYES: Self-luminous, bright red, approximately two to three inches in diameter, set wide apart. Witnesses say the eyes are set in near the top of shoulders.

6. LEGS: Man-like. No witness has ever been able to describe the feet.

7. ARMS: None. No witness has ever reported seeing arms.

8. WINGS: Fold against the back when not in use. Wingspread, everyone agrees, is about ten feet. Bat-like. Do not flap in flight.

9. CARRIAGE: Animal walks erect like a man. Does not stoop like a bear or ape. Moves its legs in a shuffling manner. Some said it "waddled."

10. SOUND: Loud squeaks, like a mouse. One witness said it sounded "like a squeaky fan belt." Two witnesses testified they heard a mechanical humming sound as the creature flew overhead.

11. SPEED: It is said to have kept pace with automobiles moving seventy to one hundred mph. Few birds can achieve this in level flight. Pilot witnesses estimated it was traveling at least seventy mph in level flight without flapping its wings.

The anomalous bird hypothesis is strongly supported by the Ohio sightings. . . . However, if the "Mothman" was the Ohio bird, then its behavior would have been different. It would not have been so illusive, since the Ohio creatures did not seem to be particularly disturbed by the presence of the witnesses. Moreover, something that looked like nothing more than a giant bird would be more apt to evoke curiosity instead of terror. It is also puzzling that no one else in Ohio or West Virginia even glimpsed such a bird. But it is possible that the gravediggers in Clendenin may have done so.

Two unusual birds were caught in the area, however. In late December 1966 a rare Arctic snow owl was shot by a farmer in Gallipolis Ferry, West Virginia. This was two feet tall and had a five foot wingspan. "Mothman" witnesses converged on the farmer for a look at the owl and all of them declared that it in no way resembled what they had seen. . . .

The winged "Mothman" never left behind any footprints, droppings or other physical evidence. The only traces of any kind that were found were some giant dog tracks. Similar tracks have been found at other monster sites around the world.

People in Point Pleasant continued to see monsters and UFOs throughout 1969, but Mrs. Hyre published very few of their reports. One morning in April 1969 Mr. Ernest Adkins stepped from his home on a farm near New Haven, West Virginia, and found his eleven-week-old beagle pup dead in his yard. "There was no evidence that the dog died in a fight," Adkins said. "But there was a large, very neat hole in its side, and the animal's heart was lying outside the body. It looked as if something chewed it out. There were no other marks on the body."

No known animal would, or could, tear the heart out of a dog without leaving other marks on the carcass. And any animal that might attempt such a thing would certainly have eaten the heart or some part of the dog.

We investigated the situation in Point Pleasant as thoroughly and as carefully as was humanly possible. But after all of our interviews and all of our experiences we were still left with the basic, disturbing question: What is really on the loose in West Virginia?

Many People Have Witnessed the *Chupacabras* and Its Work

Bucky McMahon

In the fall of 1995 in Canóvanas, Puerto Rico, more than one hundred animals—goats, chickens, dogs, and others—met mysterious, violent deaths. Many of the animals appeared to have died of a single puncture wound to the neck, and many were said to have had all their blood drained from their bodies. The evidence pointed to an unknown animal as the culprit.

These were not the first such deaths, and they wouldn't be the last. From time to time eyewitnesses caught glimpses of the killer—said to be a smallish creature with strong, kangaroo-like back legs, small front legs, and large, glowing red eyes. Witnesses reported that the creature had strange, scaly fur that appeared to change color in different light or

Bucky McMahon, "Goatsucker Sighted, Details to Follow," *Outside* magazine, www.outsideonline.com, September 1996. Copyright © 1996 by Michael R. McMahon. Reproduced by permission.

when seen against different backgrounds. The creature also appeared to have a ridge of spines along its back. Soon, the creature came to be called *el chupacabras*, "the goatsucker," because some of its early victims were goats, an important livestock animal for many Puerto Rican farmers.

Goatsucker reports spread across the island, and then appeared in Mexico, Central America, Florida, Texas, and elsewhere, primarily in Hispanic communities. The height of the *chupacabras* frenzy was from 1995 to 1996, but people have continued to report encounters with the creature—or its nasty work.

The *chupacabras* thoroughly captured the imagination of the public, leading to songs, T-shirts, and even festivals devoted to the vicious beast. While many people believe that there are more ordinary explanations for the activities attributed to the *chupacabras*, many others believe this is a creature different from any known animal. Just what the creature is is a subject of much speculation.

In the following article, Bucky McMahon describes some of the eyewitness reports and the efforts of Canóvanas mayor Jose Soto to capture the *chupacabras*. McMahon is *Outside* magazine's San Juan, Puerto Rico, bureau chief.

Canovanas, Puerto Rico—An unwelcome anniversary is being celebrated here, one that elicits not joy from the citizens of this and neighboring towns, but anxiety. It was a year ago this month [September 1995] that the residents of Guaynabo, a suburb of San Juan, awoke to a troubling scene: Strewn about in the yards of several homes were the still bodies of two rabbits, two guinea fowls, and a dozen chickens. Their necks were neatly perforated by double-fang bites, and their corpses had been drained of blood.

Two days later, in Canovanas, a small city of 37,000 people located 30 miles east of San Juan, Michael Negron, 25, discovered an agile, erect, two-legged creature hopping animatedly in the dirt outside his house. "It was about three or four feet tall, with skin like that of a dinosaur," he said. "It had eyes the size of hens' eggs, long fangs, and multicolored spikes down its head and back."

These two incidents, the first in a pattern of unusual events that have swept across Puerto Rico and much of the rest of the Western Hemisphere over the last 12 months, seemed to warrant further investigation. A few days spent not long ago questioning the citizenry of this rainforest hamlet produced the following details.

The creature seen by Mr. Negron did not display friendly behavior. The morning after the sighting, Mr. Negron's brother, Angel, 27, observed the same beast crouched over the family goat, Suerte. Attempts by Mr. Negron to roust the mysterious creature succeeded, and it retreated hastily into the jungle.

Mr. Negron then turned his attentions to Suerte, lying dead in the yard. The goat had been neatly slit open and disemboweled, its warm viscera glistening in the morning sun. Gazing upon the scene, Mr. Negron later admitted to being struck by the surgical care that had been exercised upon his goat. It was his opinion that the unfamiliar predator had been browsing expertly through the goat's entrails, looking for something.

In the months following these encounters, other sightings were reported in the vicinity of Canovanas, a densely populated city of ramshackle shacks and pastel cement homes perched on steep, lush hillsides. At least 15 people witnessed the creature. One Canovanas townsperson found his cow lying dead in a field with two punctures in its neck. Another man, who maintained a small chicken aviary on the roof of his home—guarded by the family dog, Toÿo—found the aviary plundered and the fowl dead. Later, the dog was located behind the house, trembling "in a state of fear," according to the farmer.

On another occasion, the creature paused on the sidewalk outside the home of Madelyne Tolentino, studying her as she hung her laundry out to dry. Mrs. Tolentino, 31, joined her husband and a neighbor in a hurried attempt to tackle the animal—which she described as both alien-looking and kangaroolike, with powerful hind legs and a strong sulfurous odor—but the beast managed to escape.

Disturbed by these developments, residents asked Canovanas mayor Jose Soto Rivera to mount a campaign against the animal, which had acquired the name *el chupacabras*, the goatsucker. Mr. Soto, 52, agreed. "Whatever it is, this creature is highly intelligent," he later explained to the viewing audience of *Cristina!*, a Spanish-language talk show taped in Miami. "Today it is attacking animals, but tomorrow it may attack people."

Midnight Jungle Searches

Given Mr. Soto's personal involvement with the goatsucker, his perspective seems necessary when examining how a community is affected by the invasion of a vampiric, possibly otherworldly predator. Happily, Mr. Soto agreed to sit for a lengthy interview, reclining in a leather chair at his mayoral headquarters, which occupies a prominent location on the town's shaded square.

Known locally as Chemo, a nickname from his days as a standout boxer, Mr. Soto is a quiet, ruggedly handsome man with a thin, dapper mustache. Before becoming mayor, he also pursued careers as a soldier, a mailman, and a police detective.

Mr. Soto said that on October 29 [1995], the Sunday before Halloween, he led an evening expedition of 200 Civil Defense employees and other volunteers into the dense jungle surrounding Canovanas. They dressed in camouflage and armed themselves with torches, nets, spearguns, pistols, and other weapons. Seeking to capture a live goatsucker, they erected large, metal traps, baiting them with goats and small cattle.

"We're close," Mr. Soto recalled saying, referring to his prey. "I can smell him."

Unfortunately, the goatsucker eluded the posse that evening, and it continued to do so on subsequent weekly hunts. "We've never seen him," Mr. Soto acknowledged, speaking between occasional interruptions from his cellular phone. "We can't catch him or beat him."

Rabbits Slain on Long Island

But even as Mr. Soto redoubled his efforts, the goatsucker's range grew, on a northwesterly track, with a flurry of sightings in south Florida, Texas, California, Mexico, Costa Rica, and the Dominican Republic. Reports detailing the goatsucker's movements arrived daily. Fears of imminent human casualties—the driving force behind Mr. Soto's campaigns against the creature—were realized on April 15 of this year [1996], with the first goatsucker assault on a human. Juana Tizoc, 21, received multiple bites and lacerations after being attacked by a goatsucker while strolling the fields near her family's farm in the town of Alfonso Calderon, in northern Sinaloa, Mexico. Ms. Tizoc described being set upon by the creature after it descended from the sky on weblike appendages—a detail confirming the hypothesis that several species of the creature exist, both winged and nonwinged.

On May 10, a rooster fell victim in Mendota, California, and the Fresno County Department of Agriculture subsequently logged ten complaints of goatsucker activity, prompting worried parents to cancel their children's prom outings. According to the *St. Petersburg Times*, 69 animals were attacked and killed on May 14 in the Miami neighborhood known as Sweetwater. The victims included geese, goats, chickens, and ducks. By May 17, half of Mexico's 32 states had registered attacks involving the creature.

These escalating reports led some communities in the United States to make light of the situation, an all too common reaction to unexplained phenomena. At the annual Puerto Rico Day festival in New York City, scores of paraders fashioned goatsucker costumes in an attempt to find levity in the tragedies befalling their homeland. On May 19, several pranksters in Cambridge, Massachusetts, claimed to have observed the creature, a sighting that was later determined to be specious. "I knew it was headed our way," Cambridge Chamber of Commerce staff member Alison Dowd later mused in the *Boston Herald*. "But I had no idea it was already here."

And yet that same week, out on Long Island, New York, an actual goatsucker struck the Bayshore home of Miguel Lopez, 42, dispatching a dozen chickens and seven rabbits with its classic double-fanged bite.

In the fearful months since the attack on Mr. Lopez's animal . . . goatsuckers have drained, killed, and mutilated hundreds of domestic livestock throughout the hemisphere, and, operating in increasingly brazen fashion, have effected scores of thus far nonlethal attacks on humans.

DNA Results Inconclusive

Seekers of the goatsucker typically turn to Mr. Soto for assistance and advice. Recently he entertained a group of 13 members of Beyond Boundaries, a UFO phenomena research group led by Jorge Martin, publisher of the periodical *Eviden-*

cia Ovni. Mr. Soto introduced the visiting scholars to one of his constituents, a woman who had located a goatsucker nesting site. The woman had earlier brought samples of the creature's "oddly shaped" dung and hair—with minute traces of goatsucker flesh attached—to the mayor, who promptly sent them for DNA testing. (The results proved inconclusive.)

Despite this laboratory setback, Mr. Soto perseveres, methodically stalking his prey using all techniques available to him. He maintains a thick file devoted to his adversary, with depositions from witnesses and experts, photos of the dead livestock and of the baited traps, and his own notes on the case.

The victims on Mr. Soto's conscience are many—some 200 innocent animals, several of which he was personally acquainted with, including horses, cattle, sheep, rabbits, peacocks, parakeets, a Doberman pinscher, and a rottweiler.

Mr. Soto notes that some theorists have speculated that the creature may be the product of a gene-splicing lab, the abnormal result of industrial pollution, or part of a Central Intelligence Agency plan to destabilize the region.

Mr. Soto himself believes that the goatsucker is extraterrestrial, drawn to Puerto Rico by the Arecibo Observatory, the world's largest radio telescope, which nightly receives data from the planets beyond. "In my thoughts I know this is something from another world," he said.

Recently, the mayor shared his thoughts with an American television program, *Unsolved Mysteries*, and its host, Hollywood actor Robert Stack.

Eyewitness observations, the mayor noted, have provided a profile of the creature that is highly detailed: a cock's crest atop a simian head; large, red eyes; a long, lipless mouth with a flickering reptilian tongue; small, attenuated arms that are webbed for flight and that terminate in three curved claws; and dorsal spines of iridescent beauty that are capable of changing colors, depending on the goatsucker's prevailing mood.

At the mayor's request, Dr. Carlo Soto (no relation) performed autopsies on the dead livestock, and his report tells of deep, precisely inflicted puncture wounds "inconsistent" with any known animal.

The goatsucker apparently has highly specialized teeth of the length and diameter of a common drinking straw, with the same efficient liquid-sucking qualities.

Dr. Soto observed that the goatsucker's victims show an odd resistance to rigor mortis, and what little blood remains at the crime scenes resists the ordinary tendency to coagulate, thus remaining eminently drinkable.

Observed at Close Range

Ismael Aquayo, Canovanas's Chief of Civil Defense, is a slight-framed, bespectacled public servant who now spends most of his working days pursuing the creature. On a recent muggy afternoon, he agreed to lead this reporter on a round of goatsucker-related investigations. Mr. Aquayo climbed into one of his department's large utility trucks and set out for the fern-shrouded rainforest.

Known locally as El Yunque, the rainforest is the last remaining expanse of wilderness in this densely populated commonwealth of four million people. Among the practitioners of the island's many Afro-Caribbean religions, such as Santeria and Obeah, El Yunque remains a place of mystical power. Not infrequently, foresters discover small altars alongside the rivers, speckled with blood and ceremonial wax. Sacrificed chickens, their throats slit, can be seen floating down the forest's many streams, surprising tourists and picnickers from the city of San Juan.

Arriving at Campo Rico, a barrio of 3,000 people, Mr. Aquayo turned onto a side street and parked beside a tin-roofed garage, where he spoke for a moment with Miguel Tolentino, 35, an automobile mechanic and the husband of Madelyne Tolentino, the woman who spied the creature while hanging out her laundry.

Early on the morning in question, Mr. Tolentino had just begun repairs on a truck when, opening the hood, he flushed a goatsucker from its resting place beneath the vehicle. He saw it only for a second before it leaped away. Mr. Tolentino described the goatsucker as bounding, with little apparent effort, high over the trees—a leap that was later measured at approximately 40 feet.

Later that same day the goatsucker returned to the Tolentinos' neighborhood. It paced down the street, walking upright like a man, but slightly crouched. It stopped to stare at Madelyne Tolentino with its ovoid eyes. Mrs. Tolentino boldly stared back. Because this remains the longest close-proximity sighting of the goatsucker yet recorded, proper import should be given Mrs. Tolentino's observation.

The goatsucker appeared to be about three feet tall. It was brownish to black in color and seemed to have no hair on its abdomen. Its eyes were large and jellylike, with no apparent pupils.

It was at this point that the Tolentinos rushed the animal and the goatsucker bounded away.

Mrs. Tolentino saw the goatsucker one more time—a rare second sighting—on January 2 of [1996]. She was driving home and smelled the distinct, sulfurous indicator of goatsucker activity. Then, gazing up into the sky above her, Mrs. Tolentino spotted it—the goatsucker, floating in the air, rising and dipping almost gracefully. "Like a butterfly," she said.

No End in Sight

The Tolentinos' encounter is only one of the many entries in Mr. Soto's growing dossier on the goatsucker, which on the morning after this reporter's excursion with Mr. Aquayo, was laid open across the mayor's large polished desk. Sightings and tales of the goatsucker increase daily with—to Mr. Soto's visible discomfort—no end in sight.

"As a farming community," he said, "we can't relax knowing that this goatsucker is out there killing our animals. He could take out a child, a woman, a defenseless man.". . .

"Something very strange is going on in our town," he said at the close of the interview, "and the world simply does not want to accept it." Mr. Soto then laid his hand on the goatsucker file. "This thing is not a joke."

The *Chupacabras* Is No Ordinary Predator

Jorge Martin

Jorge Martin is one of the foremost Hispanic investigators of paranormal phenomena, in particular UFOs. He is the editor of *OVNI Evidencia*, a Puerto Rican magazine devoted to UFO research. (*OVNI* is the Spanish term for *UFO*.) When reports of *chupacabras* encounters in Puerto Rico became widespread, Martin spent months investigating, interviewing witnesses, and seeking conclusive evidence to explain the phenomenon. In the following article, he sums up some of what he found and speculates about the nature of the *chupacabras*. He claims that the evidence that has been analyzed shows that the *chupacabras* could be a type of creature known as an anomalous biological entity (ABE), a creature unknown to zoologists at this time and possibly connected to UFOs.

Since December 1994, the Caribbean island of Puerto Rico has been the site of a consistent wave of UFO sightings, as well as numerous apparitions of a weird creature which has killed livestock and been dubbed the "Chupacabras" [the Goatsucker] by the sensation-seeking media. The creature is apparently responsible for the deaths of cattle, sheep, goats, rabbits, hens, ducks, cats and dogs, etc. After death, the creature appears to extract blood and other fluids from the animal's body.

Thousands of animals have been killed, and communities now live in fear. Throughout the killings, the authorities have claimed the deaths are due to attacks from groups of stray dogs, baboons or exotic animals illegally introduced in the island's territory. The director of Puerto Rico's Department of Agriculture Veterinary Services Division, Hector Garcia, has stated that, "it could be dogs, that the small puncture wounds observed in the victims' necks are similar to those inflicted by the fangs of canines." He also stated that no other unusual features have been observed in the dead animals examined by his division, and this included no loss of blood. Veterinarian Angel Luis Santana, of the private Gardenville Clinic, in San Juan, said, "it could be a human being who belongs to a religious sect, even another animal. It could also be someone who wants to make fun out of the Puerto Rican people." All of the above official 'explanations' to the enigma have failed to identify the manner in which the animals died, and the observations made of unknown creatures by serious reliable witnesses all over Puerto Rico. The facts tell a very different story. . . .

The animals have been found with many small perfect circular holes about ¼"–½" in diameter arranged in pairs of triangular fashion. These penetrate deep into the neck or lower jaws of the victims. Doctor Carlos Soto, a qualified veterinarian, states the wounds have a regular pattern in many of the cases—into the head of the animal—a hole penetrating through the right jaw bone, muscle and tissue, and straight into the brain: more specifically directly to the cerebellum, puncturing it and causing instant death to the animal. This regular type of wound, and the path followed by whatever intrudes into the body, indicates premeditation—and intelligence. Of great interest, the attack reveals a type of euthanasia technique, for this method prevents the attacked animal from suffering. This too revealed intelligence.

No Ordinary Predator

Official research fails to explain the following: If a dog or any known animal predator bites to kill a victim, it must first exert pressure on both sides of the head, neck or body.

In the "Chupacabras" case files, no trauma, abrasions, scratches, bites or pressure have been observed by the examiners on the opposite side of the wound, and as such, it becomes obvious we are not dealing with an ordinary predator/carnivore species known to science.

The wounds may be similar in appearance to bites inflicted by dogs or baboons due to them being round and small, but the similarity ends there. Government officers and veterinarians who have followed the 'official line' or policy statements have often refused to reveal data about the wounds. They conveniently ignore the fact that whatever penetrates the animal is at least three or four inches long, and in a few cases, has been known to cauterize the wall of the wound—apparently to prevent excessive blood loss. No known animal species on Earth can do this. Some of the wounds of this type appear on the sides and belly of the victim. This penetration usually cuts through the stomach—down to the liver, apparently removing sections of the organ and absorbing liquid from it. Such actions would require an incision of up to five inches—a fact verified during necropsies performed on the animals. The triangular wounds have been noted to enter the body and hit the liver.

Whilst 'something' obviously penetrates the animal, creating extensive trauma and injury, and leaving strange material inside the tissue, no natural inflammatory processes have been observed in the dead animals' tissues. This is extremely unnatural.

In most cases the victims lack rigor mortis and remain flexible—days after their death. Incredibly in some incidents, the blood which remained in the body would not clot or coagulate for days following death.

Several larger holes or cuts have been discovered on some animals. These consist of wounds which range from one inch in diameter to twelve inches in length. These particular openings have been located in the neck, chest, belly and anal areas, and appear to have been made with a surgeon's scalpel. Clean-cut openings through which certain organs are excised from the bodies. Reproductive, sexual organs, anus, eyes and other soft tissue have all been removed.

Another official explanation identifies the possibility that someone involved with a religious or satanic sect may be responsible. The sheer number of cases appears to negate this potential. The killings occur every day, at all hours, and all over the island. There is no single sect which has anything like the resources to conduct such an act. Only the government could conduct such an operation, but what possible reasons would they have to do this?

Many of the killings are associated with strange creatures we have called the Anomalous Biological Entities [ABEs]. It is reportedly a cross between a creature known as a 'Grey' alien humanoid, mainly because of the shape of its head and eyes, and what most witnesses describe as the body of a bipedal, erect dinosaur, but with no tail. Its head is oval in shape and has an elongated jaw. Two elongated red eyes have been reported, together with small holes in the nostril area, a small slit-like mouth with fang-type teeth protruding upwards and downwards from the jaw. Other witnesses have seen small pointed ears, but this feature has not been seen by other witnesses. It appears to have strong coarse hair all over its body and whilst most observers claim the hair is black, it has the remarkable ability to change colours at will, almost like a chameleon.

In the dark, it will change to black or a deep brown colour—in a sunlit area surrounded by vegetation, it changes to green, green-grey, light brown or beige.

The creature has two small arms with a three-fingered clawed hand and two strong hind legs, again with three claws. This appears to enable it to run quickly and leap over trees—some witnesses allege over twenty feet in a single bound. According to many observations, the creature's legs look almost reptilian or goat-like. It has quill-like appendages running down from the back of its head and down its back, with what seem to be fleshy membranes that change colour from blue to green, red to purple, etc. A number of witnesses claim the creature flaps (at incredible speed) its tail and appendages, allowing it to actually fly. The tail apparently is used to guide its flight only—controlled mainly by the wings—only *occasionally* seen to flap.

First reported in the town of Orocovis, the ABEs have been sighted in the municipality of Canovanas and in many areas of Puerto Rico. Its habits are both diurnal and nocturnal—as a matter of fact, it has been seen in broad daylight by several witnesses. One such occasion was witnessed by Madeline Tolentino and her neighbours in the Campo Rico community (municipality of Canovanas). They all observed it walking down a street at 3:00 PM in the afternoon. As they approached it, the creature ran away, 'at a fantastic speed,' and escaped.

The killings are a great loss to farmers, and the situation has prompted the President of the Puerto Rico House of Representatives Agricultural Commission, Mr. Juan E. [Kike] Lopez, to introduce a resolution asking for an official investigation to clarify the situation.

At this time, it has been brought to my attention that at least two of these creatures have been captured by Government officers, both from the U.S. Federal Government, and the Puerto Rican Government.

They were captured before the 6 and 7 of November [1995], one of them in the town of San Lorenzo, in the centre-east of Puerto Rico: the other in the National Caribbean Rain Forest in El Yunque, to the east.

Both were alive and allegedly taken to the United States by special personnel. Our government keeps denying the facts, yet our people perceive they are being lied to. The killings and encounters with these creatures continue. It is probably due to the fact that the incidents are associated with UFOs, that the government continues to cover-up the facts.

UFO Sightings

Luminous oval and pyramidal-shaped UFOs have been seen in the vicinity where animals have been mutilated and found to be without blood. These have been reported in the towns of Cabo Rojo, Canovanas, Ponce and Naranjito—distances apart. In Barrio Hato, the Rojas family observed a UFO. A horse and several goats were found mutilated shortly after the observation.

On 18 November 1995, a luminous disc some 40ft in diameter with a row of dark 'windows' around its centre rim positioned itself over the antennae of *Radio Procer*, a radio station located in the town of Barranquitas, in the centre of Puerto Rico. Simultaneously, the station's electronic equipment went crazy—dials just went wild. Incredibly, an obsolete piece of equipment from 1957 stored at the station turned itself on.

More astonishingly was the fact that the apparatus was *not* plugged into any power source. This incident was discussed in the media, as many residents in that area saw the UFO as it hovered over the station.

Sadly, the TV, radio and news media suppressed information on several encounters—some by residents next to the radio station. Channel 4 [WAPA TV] and Channel 11 [Tele 11] covered the incident, but failed to mention the presence of creatures during the sighting. This implies a cover-up by the media.

A female witness also observed the creature in the Canovanas municipality in the early days of November. The ABE jumped or flew and entered a round luminous object over her car.

The reports suggest a link between the ABEs and UFOs or alien phenomena. But we cannot discard the possibility that the ABEs can also be the product of highly sophisticated genetic manipulations by human agencies. A Chinese-Russian scientist by the name of Doctor Tsian Kanchen has produced genetic manipulations which have created new species of electronically-crossed plant and animal organisms. Kanchen developed an electronic system whereby he can pick up the bioenergetic field of the DNA of living organisms and transfer it electronically to other living organisms. By these means he has created incredible new breeds of ducks/chickens, with physical characteristics of both species; goats/rabbits, and new breeds of plants such as corn/wheat, peanut/sunflower seeds and cucumber/watermelons. These are produced by linking the genetic data of different living organisms contained in their bioenergetic fields by means of ultra-high frequencies biological linking.

If the Russians have created this technology, then without

doubts the US and other powers have too. Therefore, it is quite possible that the "Chupacabras" or ABEs could have been developed by humans.

Puerto Rico has been the site for much experimentation by the United States on the island's population and territory for decades. Examples of this can be found in the experimentation of Talidomida and anti-conceptive drugs on our women, which caused the birth of many malformed children in the 1950s. The lethal 'orange agent' and other dioxine-based chemical agents were tested in several places on the island, as well as gamma radiation tests in our forests. Because of this we can't exclude the "possibility" that *someone* may well have been experimenting with new and advanced genetic products in our country. The ABEs could be the result and *has* gone awry . . . who knows? Perhaps the creatures have escaped and that *someone* has lost control of the situation?

We obtained samples of blood allegedly from one of the creatures which was discovered after it jumped over a fence and tripped. This occurred at 9:00 pm on 3 October 1995, in Campo Rico, in Canovanas. Two days before, a policeman shot one of the creatures in Campo Rico which fled the site. The blood could well have been from that ABE.

We proceeded to take the blood sample to a medical specialist and hopefully for DNA analysis. These tests are currently underway in the U.S., but here are the preliminary results:

SAMPLE 1. The original blood sample seemed to indicate similar characteristics to that of human A-type blood, with Rh factor. Further analysis was not conclusive on this.

SAMPLE 2. Other analysis of the blood and matter associated to it in the sample showed a material content comparable to feces with detritus, E. Coli bacteria worms, and other parasites. Vegetal cellular material was also found. The content was comparable with that found in cases involving an injured animal or human with open wounds in the intestines, through which a blood haemorrhage was issuing.

SAMPLE 3. The genetic analysis so far has revealed that the blood is in no way compatible with human blood nor with any other blood type belonging to any animal species known to science. The traces ratio of magnesium, phosphorous, calcium and potassium are not compatible with those of normal human blood, they are much too high. The albumen/glouline [RG ratio] was not compatible either (with human blood) it was also too high. The ratios found do not allow the results of the analysis to be compatible with those of any known animal species.

At present, we can't place the sample with any earthly organism. Therefore it could well be the product of a highly sophisticated genetic manipulation, an organism alien to our own environment or perhaps extraterrestrial.

Other preliminary tests on subtypes and genetic analysis are not conclusive—yet, but the results so far imply the samples originate from an unknown organism.

Disinformation and Concealment

Obviously the alien potential would be difficult for the U.S. and Puerto Rican authorities to explain, and has led to a disinformation programme, through which government agencies disseminate the 'already discredited' official explanations of feral dogs, baboons, apes and other exotic animals or satanic cults as those capable of these actions. This has been strengthened by certain 'media jokers' who have sensationalized and made light of the situation. In many instances, ridicule has been used as a 'weapon' against serious witnesses.

Other disinformation and debunking campaigns appeared organised through UFO groups by the US intelligence services. Serious investigators have had their credibility affected. At least two groups disseminate information through the media—spreading panic as they tell of how the "Chupacabras" or ABEs belong to an alien race who 'created the AIDS' virus to destroy the human race. Another body spread fear by explaining the "Chupacabras" belong to a voracious reptilian race of creatures, alien in origin, who have started "devouring the populace." For our part, we have denounced their intent.

It is clear that *someone* apparently related to the intelligence community intends to start a panic, whilst at the same time, *someone*, for reasons unknown, is trying to prevent this alarming situation from reaching the serious parts of the media in the United States.

On one side we have the bogus UFO investigation groups created by US intelligence in Puerto Rico to disinform and intoxicate the media with ridiculous stories. Also, a crew from the US TV show *Inside Edition* visited Puerto Rico to report on the "Chupacabras" but it was obvious to everyone here that they were trying to ridicule one of the witnesses. Jose Soto, Mayor of the town of Canovanas, had a serious argument with the producers, who also tried to ridicule him. Our organisation was also subjected to silly questions. Apparently they intend to 'air' the show to discredit the situation and our research.

This is not the first occasion this particular programme has affected the credibility of our study programme; many still remember the important UFO sightings in Fyffe County, Alabama, 1990. The television programme grossly ridiculed the witnesses and case files. This should alert investigators in the United States.

The events in Puerto Rico may provide good enough reasons for discussion, and it is too important to be kept hidden from the public.

Living Pterodactyls Haunt Our Skies

David Hatcher Childress

"He's huge, he's huge, he's really, really big." So said pilot John Bouker about the gigantic bird the size of a small airplane that he and several others reported seeing flying over southwest Alaska in October 2002. According to the *Anchorage Daily News* on October 15 that year, Bouker had been skeptical when he had heard other reports of giant birds. Then he and his airplane passengers saw it for themselves. Scientists still are not sure what Bouker and others observed.

Such sightings are not as rare as you might think. They have been reported in many places from ancient times to today. Sightings vary. Some of the giants resemble known birds, such as eagles, but in sizes unimaginable. Others look very much like the long-extinct pterodactyl or pteranodon.

Could living dinosaurs exist? David Hatcher Childress, author of the following article, is convinced that they do. He even thinks pteranodons might be the explanation for another mysterious monster, the *chupacabras*, or "goatsucker," a

David Hatcher Childress, "Chupacabras and Living Pteradons," *World Explorer*, vol. 2, 2001, pp. 59–71. Copyright © 2001 by the World Explorers Club. Reproduced by permission.

small, vicious beast with kangaroo-like back legs and glowing red eyes that came to public attention in 1995 when it was declared responsible for a rash of livestock killings in Puerto Rico. In the following excerpt, Childress describes giant bird sightings and discusses his reasons for believing that these mysterious monsters might indeed be living dinosaurs.

Childress is the founder of the World Explorers Club, located in Kempton, Illinois, and publisher of *World Explorer* magazine. He has spent years traveling the world, tracking down ancient mysteries, and he has written numerous books and magazine articles on such topics.

Reports of strange flying reptiles, some quite large, have continued well into modern times. As we shall see, reports of pteranodons, dragons, thunderbirds, and other similar monsters, are relatively common. Could the sudden rash of Chupacabras attacks and sightings be related to the occasional rash of pteranodon sightings?

Many of the aspects of the Chupacabras and living pteranodons seem to match. They are both monsters and flesh eaters. Pteranodons may well drink blood and gorge themselves on internal organs, which are easy to eat. Carrion birds such as vultures and condors eat the exposed softer flesh first, lips, eyes, underbelly, etc. It would seem natural for pteranodons to do this as well. Admittedly, the Chupacabras' supposed habit of draining all the blood from two small holes on the neck, similar to the familiar vampires of lore, seems more fiction than reality. In Chile, animals were actually disappearing or being half eaten. Pteranodons are vicious meat eaters with very sharp teeth and claws to rip open victims. They apparently feed at night, much like owls. Their survival in the mountains of northern

Mexico and the southern Andes has been theorized for decades by cryptozoologists.

Giant bats, huge super-eagles called "pteratorns" and weird "mothmen" have all been put forward as explanations of these various reports. Now I come forward to state, unequivocably, that I believe these legends and sightings can be attributed to still-living flying dinosaurs—to pterodactyls or, more precisely, pteranodons.

We know that these creatures once existed because of the fossil record. Sightings have continued to this day, and legends abound, but where is the physical evidence that these creatures still exist? One thing that must be first understood is that fossils are anomalous geological artifacts, typically made because of some cataclysm or volcanic disaster. Most animals when they die, naturally or by a predator, simply decay and return to dust. The point here is that a pterodactyl that died in a desert or jungle or mountain crag 1,000 years ago (or even 10) would not have left a fossil behind for us to prove to us that it had been there.

The second thing that must be understood about these amazing flying animals is that they are nocturnal and live only in extremely remote and uninhabited areas of the earth. Even so, there are literally hundreds of reports of giant birds and flying lizards showing up around the world. The most amazing pteranodon fossil ever discovered was at Big Bend National Park in Texas. The park was the site of the discovery of the skeleton of a giant pteranodon in 1975. It had a wingspan of 51 feet and is the largest fossil of a flying reptile so far discovered. Other pterodactyls were much smaller and had wingspans from 8 to 20 feet.

Though pteranodons are believed to have become extinct about 65 million years ago, this may not necessarily be the case. Many creatures which lived at that time are still alive, such as crocodiles, turtles, and the famous coelacanth [prehistoric fish]. Even the date of the fossil of the giant pteranodon found at Big Bend is in question. Since fossils cannot be dated by any known technical method, their age is guessed at from the geological strata around them, and since the current dating of geological strata is based on the prevailing Uniformitarian theory of slow geological change, the date of many fossils may be radically closer to our own than 65 million years.

Legends of Flying Reptiles

The Chinese have had legends for thousands of years of flying reptiles called dragons, and flying snakes as well—something apparently different. Flying reptile dragon images in China are so prevalent, they can easily be considered amongst the most common of motifs. Are they stylized depictions of real flying animals? The ancient Chinese certainly thought they were.

Similarly, most countries of Europe and the Mediterranean have myths and legends of heroes battling flying reptiles—or dragons. Often depicted as winged snakes or winged alligators, these dragons were a common image as well, and are still used in the crests of royal families. Did dragons—flying reptiles—pterodactyls—still exist in small numbers, even up to the Middle Ages?

Almost every Indian tribe from Alaska to Tierro del Fuego has legends of a gigantic flying monster so large that, ". . . it darkened the sun." The clapping of these giants' wings created thunder, so they were known as "Thunderbirds." The Navajo Indians still perform their Thunderbird dance, and tell the legends of the "cliff monster" which lived in a high craggy roost, descending to carry people off to feed to its young. The Haida natives of the Queen Charlotte Islands of British Columbia believe that some Thunderbirds were so large that they could literally pick up small whales from the sea. Much of their art and woodcarving depicts exactly such a capture by a Thunderbird.

Some South American Indians believed that the bird was constantly at war with the powers living beneath the sea, particularly a horned serpent, and that it tore open large trees in search of a giant grub which was its favorite food.

It has been suggested that the Thunderbird is in fact a living fossil—a pteranodon. Though few in number, especially these days, pterosaurs may have survived in small numbers in remote desert and mountain areas. Though it seems incredible, as I have stated, reports of "giant birds" and pteranodons continue to this day from around the world.

Pterodactyls in South America

Persistent legends and stories abound in South America of giant winged creatures. These stories have been told since before the Conquistadors arrived, and some seem to be based on far more recent sightings. The following article appeared in a magazine called *The Zoologist* in July, 1868, dateline Copiapo, Chile, April 1868: "Yesterday, at about five o'clock in the afternoon when the daily labours in this mine were over, and all the workmen were together awaiting their supper, we saw coming through the air, from the side of the ternera a gigantic bird, which at first sight we took for one of the clouds then partially darkening the atmosphere, supposing it to have been separated from the rest by the wind. Its course was from north-west to south-east; its flight was rapid and in a straight line. As it was passing a short distance above our heads we could mark the strange formation of its body. Its immense wings were clothed with something resembling the thick and stout bristles of a boar, while on its body, elongated like that of a serpent, we could only see brilliant scales which clashed together with metallic sound as the strange animal turned its body in its flight."

Also in South America, a Mr. J. Harrison of Liverpool said that when he was navigating an estuary of the Amazon in 1947 called Manuos, he and others observed from the boat's deck a flight of five huge birds passing overhead and down the river in a V-formation. But they were no ordinary birds, said Mr. Harrison in a letter: "The wingspan must have been at least twelve feet from tip to tip. They were brown in colour like brown leather, with no visible signs of feathers. The head was flat on top, with a long beak and a long neck. The wings were ribbed." He said that the creatures "were just like those large prehistoric birds."

Airplane-Pterodactyl Encounter?

A similar incident in South America was published in 1992 by the Australian weekly magazine *People*. In this encounter, a small commuter aircraft nearly crashed into a giant flying lizard over the mountain jungles of Brazil. A U.S. anthropologist named Dr. George Biles was supposedly aboard the plane of 24 passengers and was quoted as saying, "This was a classic case of a white pterodactyl with a giant wingspan. Of course, I've heard the rumors for many years that these prehistoric creatures still roamed the Amazon. But I was skeptical like everybody else. But that wasn't an airplane or a UFO flying beside us. It was a pterodactyl."

The *People* story says that the pterodactyl was flying alongside the plane as it was preparing to land and that the pilot veered away to avoid colliding with the "giant bird." A stewardess named Maya Cabon is quoted as saying, "Here was this giant monster flying right next to the plane. He was only a few feet away from the window—and he looked right at me. I thought we were all going to die." No actual size is given in the story, and tales like this start becoming suspect when the pilot is quoted as saying ". . . he was coming straight at us and he was mighty big!". . .

The Feathered Serpent

In the mythology and religion of Central America there is the very real tradition of Quetzalcoatl, of the Feathered Serpent (While Quetzalcoatl was a man, or series of men, he was named after the "feathered serpent."). Was there such an animal at one time—a flying reptile? Biologists say yes, pterosaurs or pteranodons, but they have been extinct for millions of years. Or have they? And could they be one possible explanation for some of the Chupacabras sightings?

Film of a pterodactyl flying over the Yucatan was widely viewed in the early 1970s, according to famous cryptozoologist Loren Coleman in his book, *Mysterious America*. Carvings of what appear to be pteranodons can be found in Mayan ruins at Tajin, located in northeastern Vera Cruz state in Mexico.

Under the title "Serpent-Bird of the Mayans," *Science Digest* published a brief article in its November, 1968 issue on the subject of a pteranodon being possibly carved into a wall at the pyramid of Tajin. Says the article, "An ancient Mayan relief sculpture of a peculiar bird with reptilian characteristics has been discovered in Totonacapan, in northeastern section of Veracruz, Mexico. Jose Diaz-Bolio, a Mexican archaeologist-journalist responsible for the discovery, says there is evidence that the serpent-bird sculpture, located in the ruins of Tajin, is not merely the product of Mayan flights of fancy, but a realistic representation of an animal that lived during the period of the ancient Mayans—1,000 to 5,000 years ago.

"If indeed such serpent-birds were contemporary with the ancient Mayan culture, the relief sculpture represents a startling evolutionary oddity. Animals with such characteristics are believed to have disappeared 130 million years ago. The acrhaeornis and the archaeopteryx, to which the sculpture bears a vague resemblance, were flying reptiles that became extinct during the Mesozoic age of dinosaurs.

"And since man did not appear, according to current geological charts, until about one million years ago, there appears to be a 129-million-year discrepancy. The twain (Mayan and serpent bird) never should have met. But Jose Diaz-Bolio is continuing his investigation, and he says that he knows of the existence of a serpent-bird skull that may hold a clue to the mystery once it has been identified."

The idea that the "feathered serpent" of the Mayas was a real animal has been a popular subject over the years. The concept that the Mayan feathered serpent was a long-necked flying reptile was used in the 1946 film *The Flying Serpent* starring George Zucco (featured in the Adventures Unlimited video *Dinosaurs Alive!*) and more recently in the 1982 David Carradine film *Q—The Winged Serpent*. The "Q" stands for the Mayan word Quetzalcoatl, or "feathered serpent." While these grade-B movies have made little impact on audiences, they do show that the idea of flying serpents—also called pteranodons—are a popular belief along the Mexican border.

The Lost Pterodactyl Photo

According to the Fortean investigator John Keel, more than 20 people have written to him claiming to have seen a photo of a dead pterodactyl nailed to the side of a building in Tombstone, Arizona. Keel claims that he has seen this photo, too, but no one can remember where!

In his column "Beyond the Known" in the March 1991 issue of *Fate* magazine, Keel discusses this intriguing photograph at length. He also quotes from a letter from the son of a Pennsylvania man named Robert Lyman who had written numerous articles and books about the weird and the unknown. Lyman wrote about Thunderbirds in one of his books entitled *Amazing Indeed*: "About 1900, two prospectors shot and carried into Tombstone, Arizona, one of these birds. When nailed against the wall of the Tombstone Epitaph building its wingspread measured 36 feet. A photograph showed six men standing under the bird with outstretched arms touching. One of them said: 'Shucks, there is no such bird, never was and never will be.' I saw that picture in a daily paper. Many other persons remember seeing it. No one has been able to find it in recent years. Two copies were at Hammersley Fork only a few years ago. One burned in a home. The other was taken away by strangers.". . .

"Officer, There's a Pterodactyl in My Backyard!"

That there were sightings of pterodactyls in the 1800s, I have no doubt. In fact the sightings in the Sonora Desert continue to this day. In the early months of 1976, a rash of "flying reptile" sightings were reported in the Rio Grande River Valley along the Mexican-American border.

One of the first encounters was in the early hours of December 26, 1975 when a rancher named Joe Suárez discovered that a goat he had tied up in a corral in Raymondville, Texas (about 30 miles north of the Rio Grande in southeastern Texas), had been ripped to pieces and partially eaten by some unknown assailant. The goat had been mauled from the right side and was lying in a pool of blood with the heart and lungs missing with the snout bitten away. The blood was still wet and warm when police officers examined the carcass. They could find no footprints around the goat and concluded that a flying creature of unknown origin had caused the death.

Then, in the same town, on January 14, 1976 at about 10:30 in the evening on the north side of Raymondville, a young man named Armando Grimaldo was sitting in the backyard of his mother-in-law's house when he was attacked by a strange winged creature.

"As I was turning to go look over on the other side of the house," said Armando to the Raymondville press, "I felt something grab me, something with big claws. I looked back and saw it and started running. I've never been scared of nothing before but this time I really was. That was the most scared I've ever been in my whole life."

This strange flying attacker had dived out of the sky—and it was something Grimaldo described as being about six feet tall with a wingspread he estimated as being from ten to twelve feet. Its skin was blackish-brown, leathery and featherless. It had huge red eyes.

Grimaldo was terrified. He screamed and tried to run but tripped and fell face first into the dirt. As he struggled up to continue running for his mother-in-law's house, the beast's claws continued to attempt to grasp him securely, tearing his clothes, which were now virtually ripped to shreds. He managed to dive under a bush and the attacking animal, now breathing heavily, flew away into the sky.

Grimaldo then crashed into the house, collapsing on the floor, muttering "pájaro" (Spanish for bird) over and over again. He was taken to the hospital, treated for shock and minor wounds, and released.

Blazing Red Eyes

A short time later, in nearby Brownsville, on the Rio Grande, a similar creature slammed into the mobile home of Alverico Guajardo on the outskirts of town. Alverico went outside his trailer to investigate the crash into his house. When he noticed a large animal next to the crash site, he got into his station wagon and turned the lights on to see the creature, which he later described as "something from another planet."

As soon as the lights hit it, the thing rose up and glared

at him with blazing red eyes. Alverico, paralyzed with fear, could only stare back at the creature whose long, batlike wings were wrapped around its shoulders. All the while it was making a "horrible-sounding noise in its throat." Finally, after two or three minutes of staring into the headlights of the station wagon, it backed away to a dirt road a few feet behind it and disappeared in the darkness.

These were just the first of a number of bizarre encounters with seemingly prehistoric "birds." Also in January of 1976, two sisters, Libby and Deany Ford, spotted a huge and strange "big black bird" by a pond near Brownsville. The creature was as tall as they were and had a "face like a bat." They later identified it out of a book of prehistoric animals as a pteranodon.

The *San Antonio Light* newspaper reported on February 26, 1976, that three local school teachers were driving to work on an isolated road to the south of the city on February 24 when they saw an enormous bird sweeping low over cars on the road. It had a wingspan of 15–20 feet and leathery wings. It did not so much fly, as glide. They said that it was flying so low that when it swooped over the cars its shadow covered the entire road.

As the three watched this huge flying creature, they saw another flying creature off in the distance circling a herd of cattle. It looked, they thought, like an "oversized seagull." They later scanned encyclopedias at their school, and identified the creature as a pteranodon.

The sightings of flying reptiles over Texas subsided for a while, but then on September 14, 1982, James Thompson, an ambulance technician from Harlingen, saw a "birdlike object" pass over Highway 100 at a distance of 150 feet or more above the pavement. The time was 3:55 in the morning, and this huge flying creature was obviously a night hunter.

"I expected him to land like a model airplane," Thompson

told the *Valley Morning Star*, the local Rio Grande newspaper. "That's what I thought he was, but he flapped his wings enough to get above the grass. It had a black or grayish rough texture. It wasn't feathers. I'm quite sure it was a hide-type covering. I just watched him fly away." It was as the others had described the same flying creature: a "pterodactyl-like bird."

Diving "Big Bird"?

Fortean writers Loren Coleman and Jerome Clark made extensive investigations of the "Big Bird" sightings in Texas and later published their results in the book *Creatures of the Goblin World*. They chronicle all of the above incidents, and a number of others. They even obtained fecal matter from what was thought to be a pterodactyl. Although they report that the fecal matter was being analyzed, they do not give the results.

Coleman and Clark also tell the strange story of James Rowe, a retired Corpus Christi newsman, who recalled the story of a man who ran a grocery store along Corpus Christi Beach. The unnamed man was fishing along the Nueces River before the Wesley Seale Dam was built (1958) when something grabbed his hook and took off downstream. The thing almost took all of his line before he got it turned around, then it headed upstream just as far.

"He fought it and fought. Then finally the thing just climbed out of the water on a sandbar across the river from where he was standing. It was this creature with fur and feathers and it just took the hook out of its mouth. Then it climbed up a tree.

"The fellow had a pistol in his tackle box, so he took it out and started to shoot at the animal. Then as he took aim, the thing just flew away."

While this may sound like a Texas tall tale, it is curious to note here that tales of the Kongamato in Zaire/Congo/Angola also mention that the animal goes underwater and can fly as well, similar to loons, grebes, pelicans and other birds. It sounds bizarre, but then, why would people make up this unusual bit of information concerning these "monsters"?

Strange Tracks

The above stories aside, other tales were taken more seriously, even by the police. Unlike most of the others, one incident took place in daylight hours on January 1, 1976, near Harlingen, Texas. Two children, Tracey Lawson, 11, and her cousin Jackie Davies, 14, were playing in the Lawsons' backyard while their parents slept off the excesses of New Year's Eve. The two children were playing in a large backyard that faced a plowed field five miles south of Harlingen along Ed Carey Road.

Suddenly, Tracey noticed something standing a hundred yards away. Dashing inside, she picked up a pair of binoculars and returned to focus on a "horrible-looking" huge black bird. She described it as over five feet tall with big, dark red eyes, with wings bunched up at its shoulders, which were three feet wide. Its face was grey in color and "gorilla-like." It had a beak, however, that was sharp, thick, and at least six inches long. The head was bald. On one occasion during the sighting the thing made a loud, shrill "eeeee" sound.

The children were amazed and frightened. The creature suddenly disappeared, apparently flying low over a quarry or "borrow pit" along an irrigation canal, and then reappeared on the northeast corner of the property, its head poking above a small clump of trees. The children, more and more frightened, went inside the house and stayed. Later, the parents were disinclined to believe the story they were told upon awakening, but the next day Jackie's stepfather, Tom Waldon, went to the Lawson property to look for tracks to satisfy his stepson. To his surprise, he found several three-toed tracks from some unknown creature.

The first three tracks were close to the fence behind the house. The fourth print was 20 yards out into the field, and the fifth 20 yards beyond that. The tracks were three-toed, eight inches across, square at the head, and were pressed an inch and a half into the hard ground. Later, after the police and Stan Lawson arrived, the entire group examined the prints and decided that the children had been telling the bizarre truth.

Stan Lawson, who weighed 170 pounds, pressed his own foot down alongside the bird print and found it made practically no impression. "That thing must have been pretty heavy," he said later.

Coleman and Clark also mention that Stan Lawson had noticed something strange about their dog's behavior. All day it cowered inside the doghouse leaving it only once, at suppertime, when Lawson went to feed it and it bolted through the door into the main house. It had to be dragged back outside. And that night, around 10:00, Lawson heard something like large wings scraping across his bedroom window screen, but he saw nothing. In the morning he found that the screen was torn.

One puzzling part of the information is the frequent report that these strange, flying creatures have a face like a gorilla, monkey or a man. Even with a beak, it seems to have a short, flat face, rather than a long narrow pointed head as we typically associate with pterodactyls. However, some pteranodons had short, flat faces, and some had no beak whatsoever. For instance, a pterosaur known as the Anurognathus had a stubby face and sharp teeth; the Batrachognathus had a flat face, forward claws and extremely sharp teeth. Such a creature was perfectly suited for eating a goat, or even a larger animal. It would also have the appearance of a gorilla with a beak. . . .

Remote Nests in the Desert?

It seems likely that if Thunderbirds/pterodactyls live in this day and age, they must be nesting in some pretty remote and probably mountainous area. The most likely area for any concentration of flying lizards still surviving would have to be in the Sonora Desert in Mexico, just south of Arizona and New Mexico. From this area it would be quite possible for pterodactyls to still live largely undisturbed and unseen by civilization. Mexico's Sierra Madre Oriental, only 200 miles east of the Rio Grande sightings, is one of the least explored regions of North America. Flying reptiles or huge birds could still live in such a region, especially if they were mainly nocturnal.

Bibliography

Creatures of the Goblin World, Jerome Clark and Loren Coleman, 1978, Clark Publications, Chicago.

Lost Cities of North & Central America, David Hatcher Childress, 1994, Adventures Unlimited Press, Kempton, IL.

Megagods, Jim Woodman, 1987, Pocket Books, New York.

The Mothman Prophecies, John Keel, 1975, Signet Books, New York.

Mysterious America, Jerome Clark and Loren Coleman, 1983, Faber & Faber, Boston.

Mystery in Acambaro, Charles Hapgood, 2000, Adventures Unlimited Press, Kempton, IL.

The Dover Demon Is an Unsolved Mystery

Jerome Clark and Loren Coleman

Just about every area of the world has its own mysterious monster stories. In Dover, Massachusetts, a puzzling creature was reported during only one brief period, but the Dover Demon has become part of the permanent lore of the area.

According to cryptozoologist Loren Coleman, 1977 was an unusually eventful year for strange occurrences. UFO and creature sightings were abnormally frequent and often seemed to be connected; they often occurred in closely related times and places. Many of the creature sightings involved mysterious monsters with humanlike forms. People wondered if some of these creatures were from outer space. When Coleman heard reports of a mysterious monster sighted near Dover in April of that year, he went to investigate.

The following selection describes what the witnesses saw and how Coleman investigated. The selection is taken from *Creatures of the Outer Edge*, by Coleman and Jerome Clark.

Jerome Clark and Loren Coleman, *Creatures of the Outer Edge*. New York: Warner Books, 1978. Copyright © 1978 by Jerome Clark and Loren Coleman. All rights reserved. Reproduced by permission.

Both men have spent many years investigating paranormal events and have written numerous books and articles about such topics. Their most recent collaboration is *Cryptozoology A to Z*, an encyclopedia of mysterious monsters and related topics. Coleman is a professor at the University of Southern Maine, author of *Bigfoot Across America* and other books, and operates a website, "The Cryptozoologist" (www.lorencoleman.com). Clark is the author of several books, including *Unexplained! Strange Sightings, Incredible Occurrences, and Puzzling Physical Phenomena*, and is the editor of *International UFO Reporter*, published by the Center for UFO Research.

Dover, the wealthiest town in Massachusetts, is fifteen miles southwest of Boston. Although it is heavily wooded and its houses are spaced several hundred feet apart, it is hardly a place in which one would expect to encounter a strange creature unknown to science, but that's exactly what four teenagers claim they saw over a 25½-hour period in April 1977.

Eyes Like "Orange Marbles"

The bizarre affair began at 10:30 on the evening of April 21 as three seventeen-year-olds, Bill Bartlett, Mike Mazzocca and Andy Brodie, were driving north on Dover's Farm Street. Bartlett, who was behind the wheel, spotted something creeping along a low wall of loose stones on the left side of the road. At first he thought it was a dog or a cat until his headlights hit the thing directly and Bartlett realized it was nothing he had ever seen before.

The figure slowly turned its head and stared into the light, its two large, round, glassy, lidless eyes shining brightly "like two orange marbles." Its watermelon-shaped head, resting at the top of a thin neck, was fully the size of the rest of the body. Except for its oversized head, the creature was thin, with long spindly arms and legs, and large hands and feet. The skin was hairless and peach-colored and appeared to have a rough texture ("like wet sandpaper," Bill subsequently told [cryptozoologist] Loren Coleman).

The figure, which stood no more than three and a half to four feet tall, was shaped like "a baby's body with long arms and legs." It had been making its way uncertainly along the wall, its long fingers curling around the rocks, when the car lights surprised it.

Unfortunately neither of Bill's companions saw the creature. Mike was watching his own side of the road, and Andy was sitting in back talking with him. The sighting lasted only a few seconds and before Bill could speak he had passed the scene. Mike and Andy told Coleman, however, that their friend was "pretty scared" and sounded "genuinely frightened." At first they were skeptical but Bill's obvious fear forced them to change their minds.

"I really flew after I saw it," Bill said. "I took that corner at 45, which is pretty fast. I said to my friends, 'Did you see that?' And they said, 'Nah, describe it.' I did and they said, 'Go back. Go back!' And I said, 'No way. No way.' When you see something like that, you don't want to stand around and see what it's going to do.

"They finally got me to go back and Mike was leaning out of the window yelling, 'Come on, creature!' And I was saying, 'Will you cut that out?' Andy was yelling, 'I want to see you!'"

But the creature was gone. Bill dropped his friends off and went home. He was visibly upset as he walked through the door and his father asked him what was wrong. Young Bartlett related the story, then withdrew to sketch what he had seen.

"Who Is That?"

In the meantime, another teenager was about to see the creature. Around midnight John Baxter, fifteen, left his girl-friend Cathy Cronin's house at the south end of Millers High Road in Dover and started walking up the street on his way home. Half an hour later, after he had walked about a mile, he observed someone approaching him. Because the figure was quite short, John assumed it was an acquaintance of his, M.G. Bouchard, who lived on the street. John called out, "M.G., is that you?"

There was no response. But John and the figure contin-ued to approach each other until finally the latter stopped. John then halted as well and asked, "Who is that?" The sky was dark and overcast and he could see only a shadowy form.

Trying to get a better look he took one step forward and the figure scurried off to the left, running down a shallow wooded gully and up the opposite bank. As it ran John could hear its footfalls on the dry leaves.

He followed the thing down the slope, then stopped and looked across the gulley. The creature—for now John could see that was what it was—stood in silhouette about thirty feet away, its feet "molded" around the top of a rock several feet from a tree. It was leaning toward the tree and had the long fingers of both hands entwined around the trunk, which was eight inches in diameter, as if for support.

The creature's body reminded John of a monkey's, except for its dark "figure-eight"–shaped head. Its eyes, two lighter spots in the middle of the head, were looking straight at John, who after a few minutes began to feel decidedly uneasy. Realizing that he had never seen or heard of such a creature before and fearing what it might do next, he backed carefully up the slope, his heart pounding, and "walked very fast" down the road to the intersection at Farm Street. There a couple passing in a car picked him up and drove him home.

The next day Bill Bartlett told his close friend Will Taintor, eighteen, of his sighting. And that night—around midnight—Taintor himself would catch a fleeting glimpse of the creature.

A Third Sighting

[Will] was driving Abby Brabham, fifteen, home when the encounter took place. As they passed along Springdale Avenue, Abby spotted something in the headlights on the left side of the road. The "something" was a creature crouched on all fours and facing the car. Its body was thin and monkeylike but its head was large and oblong, with no nose, ears or mouth. The thing was hairless and its skin was tan or beige in color. The facial area around the eyes was lighter and the eyes glowed *green*. Abby insisted this was the case, even after investigators told her that Bill Bartlett had said the eyes were orange.

Will saw the creature only momentarily and had the impression of something with a large head and tan body, with its front legs in the air. He didn't know what it was but he did know that it was not a dog.

Frightened, Abby urged him to speed up so that they could get away. Will claims that only after they left the scene did he recall Bill's sighting. His own had been so brief and unspectacular that he probably would have thought little of it if Abby had not been with him. He asked her to describe the figure, deliberately phrasing misleading questions about aspects of the creature's appearance he knew not to be true in order to check her story against Bartlett's, which he did not mention to her. But Abby stuck to her story.

On April 28, Loren Coleman, then living in nearby Needham, was visiting the Dover Country Store when a store employee, Melody Fryer, told him about Bill Bartlett's sighting and sketch. She promised to get him a copy and two days later provided him with two drawings. The next day Coleman interviewed Bartlett. On May 3 he questioned Baxter and Brabham and on the 5th talked with Taintor.

Two weeks later Coleman pulled in Walter Webb of the Aerial Phenomena Research Organization, Joseph Nyman of the Mutual UFO Network and Ed Fogg of the New England UFO Study Group to join the investigation. Although none of the witnesses had reported seeing a UFO in connection with the Dover Demon, the ufologists were struck by the creature's apparent resemblance to humanoid beings sometimes associated with UFOs.

Honest Witnesses

The investigators interviewed the witnesses' parents, who said they believed the stories. The Bartletts said their son is "very honest and open" and not the kind of person who enjoys playing pranks. Mrs. Baxter remarked that her son "never made up stories"—meaning, apparently, that he never made up stories which he passed off as true; his father told a reporter that his son writes science fiction. But he still didn't question John's honesty. John confirmed that he is a science fiction enthusiast but insisted that had nothing to do with his report.

Will Taintor's father and mother both accepted his story. The father believed Will and Abby had mistaken a conventional animal for the creature; the mother, on the other hand, felt they had seen something genuinely unknown.

Alice Stewart, who owned the land closest to the spot where John Baxter allegedly saw the Demon, said she had not seen or heard anything unusual that night. Her dogs, which were inside at the time of the reported encounter, had not acted up.

Dover Police Chief Carl Sheridan spoke highly of young

Bartlett and described him as "a reliable witness." High school principal Richard Wakely told Coleman, "I don't think these kids got together and invented it." They were not troublemakers—just "average students." A police officer said, "At first I was going to ask one of the witnesses to give me whatever it was he was smoking, but I know all four and I know that to all of us they're very reputable people."

On April 25, four days after the first sighting, Robert Linton, science instructor at Dover-Sherborn Regional High School, overheard Bill Bartlett discussing the encounter with classmates. Later Linton asked him about it and the youth provided a full account and drew a picture of the thing. (Bartlett is an accomplished artist and a member of Boston's Copley Art Society.) Linton, who said Bill had told him that the experience "scared the hell out of him," accepted the story because of the young man's good reputation.

The researchers were especially impressed with Bartlett and with Abby Brabham, who declared adamantly, "I know I saw the creature and don't care what happens!"

Not a Hoax

Is the Dover Demon a hoax? The investigators concluded that was possible, but doubted that this was the explanation. There was nothing in the witnesses' backgrounds to suggest they might be pranksters and much to suggest that they were honest, upright individuals.

As Webb observes, "None of the four was on drugs or drinking at the time of his or her sighting so far as we were able to determine. . . . None of the principals in this affair made any attempt to go to the newspapers or police to publicize their claims. Instead, the sightings gradually leaked out. Finally, the teenagers' own parents, the high school principal, the science instructor and other adults in Dover whose comments were solicited didn't believe the Dover

Demon was a fabrication, implying the youths did indeed see 'something'. . . .

"As for the idea the witnesses were victims of somebody else's stunt, this seems most unlikely, chiefly due to the virtual impossibility of creating an animated, lifelike 'demon' of the sort described."

But if the Demon is real, what is it? A UFO being? Perhaps—but then nothing precisely similar has ever been reported before, according to Ted Bloecher, who has collected over 1500 UFO-occupant accounts for the Center for UFO Studies.

On the other hand, maybe the Demon is a member of a curious race known to the Cree Indians of eastern Canada as the *Mannegishi*. The *Mannegishi*, [naturalist] Sigurd Olson says in his book *Listening Post*, are supposed to be "little people with round heads and no noses who live with only one purpose: to play jokes on travelers. The little creatures have long spidery legs, arms with six-fingered hands, and live between rocks in the rapids. . . ."

Chapter 2

Fact or Fiction?

Mysterious
Monsters
Do Not Exist

"Mothman" Is a Barn Owl

Joe Nickell

For a brief period from 1966 to 1967, people in Point Pleasant, West Virginia, were plagued by sightings of a scary creature, a winged man that came to be called Mothman. Mothman has also been reported sporadically there and in other places since that time. Although many people claim to have seen Mothman, skeptics are convinced that there is a normal explanation for the appearances of the seemingly abnormal creature. Skeptic Joe Nickell, a senior research fellow for the Committee for the Scientific Investigation of Claims of the Paranormal (CSICOP), explains in the following article why he believes that witnesses who thought they saw Mothman actually saw the common barn owl.

Nickell also mentions the "Men in Black." Often, Mothman witnesses and witnesses to other strange phenomena, such as UFOs, claim to have been contacted and sometimes threatened by mysterious men who purport to be government agents. People in the field of paranormal investigation call these men the "Men in Black" because they usually wear

Joe Nickell, "'Mothman' Solved!" *Skeptical Inquirer*, March 2002, pp. 20–21.

black suits and hats and dark glasses.

Nickell is a regular writer for the *Skeptical Inquirer*, CSICOP's monthly magazine, and has made a career out of investigating and debunking supposedly paranormal phenomena. He is the author of several books on paranormal topics, including *Real Life X-Files: Investigating the Paranormal* and *Mysterious Realms: Probing Paranormal, Historical, and Forensic Enigmas.*

A 2002 movie, *The Mothman Prophecies*, tells the stories of a reporter (played by Richard Gere) who is drawn to a West Virginia town by eyewitness accounts of a flying monster. From November 1966 to November 1967, residents in the vicinity of Point Pleasant (near the Ohio state line) were frightened by "Mothman" (whose appellation was a reporter's takeoff on the then-current *Batman* TV series). The movie is based on a book of the same title by arch paranormal mystery monger John A. Keel (1975). Keel rounded up giant bird reports, both local and worldwide, and combined them with UFO sightings, visits by Men in Black, telephone predictions from alleged extraterrestrials and their "contactees" (precursors of the "abductees"), plus a tragic bridge collapse and sundry other elements.

"Mothman" was encountered one night about seven miles from town when two couples drove through an abandoned complex popularly called the TNT area (after its World War II use for making munitions). About 11:30 P.M., they saw the glowing red eyes of a creature, "shaped like a man, but bigger," one witness would say. "And it had big wings folded against its back." It was further described as greyish and walking on sturdy legs with a shuffling gait. As it took flight and seemed to follow them, it "wasn't even flapping its wings" but "squeaked like a big mouse" (quoted in Keel 1975, 52–53).

Soon others were seeing the winged enigma, including two Point Pleasant firemen who visited the TNT area just three nights after the couple's sighting. They too saw the red eyes and described the creature as "huge" but were emphatic: "It was definitely a bird" (Keel 1975, 56). Most reports described it as headless yet with large, shining red eyes set near the top of its body. Not all accounts agreed, however: One woman stated that what she saw "had a funny little face" although she "didn't see any beak," just those "big red poppy eyes." Keel also describes some "gigantic birds" about seventy miles to the north, in Ohio, that had a ten-foot wingspan and heads with "a reddish cast," yet lacking "the famous glowing red eyes" (Keel 1975, 60–61).

Allowing for an exaggeration of size—perhaps caused by an overestimate of the intervening distance—the Ohio birds seem to fit the appearance of the common turkey vulture which can have a six-foot wingspan and an unfeathered red head (*Audubon* 1977).

What About the Red Eyes?

But what about the red-eyed "Mothman" sightings? The creature at the old munitions area "had two big eyes like automobile reflectors," and others echoed that description, including one man who, alerted by his dog in the direction of his hay barn, spotted it with a flashlight (Keel 1975, 49, 52). Revealingly, according to Frank B. Gill's *Ornithology* (1994), "At night some birds' eyes shine bright red in the beam of a flashlight or automobile headlights. This 'eyeshine' is not the iris color but that of the vascular membrane—the tapetum—showing through the translucent pigment layer on the surface of the retina."

At this point it seems relevant to consider a real West Virginia winged creature—one that has "nocturnal habits" and "large, staring eyes" of the type that yield crimson eyeshine, plus "facial discs" that can make the eyes appear even larger. It has a large head and (unbirdlike) is "monkey-faced," but looks "quite neckless" (its very short neck sloping into its body so it could seem headless in silhouette). It has "oversized wings and long legs," the latter being "powerful" and (unlike the spindly legs of many birds) covered with feathers, making them look relatively thick. Its flight is "noiseless" and indeed "mothlike," although during flight it may vocalize a "loud, trailing 'khree-i.'" Its broad range includes West Virginia, and it is a "widespread nester in human habitations"; in fact it "hides in old buildings" (like those of the TNT complex), as well as barns, etc. Because it is active only at night, it is "seldom disturbed or even seen by humans," so when it is encountered it has an unfamiliar as well as "sinister appearance" (Bent 1961; Cerny 1975; Coe 1994; Peterson 1957, 1980; Steward 1977).

Its name is *Tyto alba*, the common barn owl. While it is far from man-sized, due to its big wings (some forty-four inches) and long legs it nevertheless "appears deceptively large, especially in flight" ("barn" 2001; Coe 1994). Allowing for such deception—compounded by multiple unknowns (distance, true size, size of nearby objects for comparison), as well as darkness, surprise, fear, and other magnification factors—we have what I believe is the most likely candidate for "Mothman." (Of course, given the many reports, there is unlikely to be a single explanation for all, and hoaxes, hallucinations, other birds, etc., may have been involved in the contagion.)

Unreliable, Excited Eyewitnesses

We are thus faced with a choice between a plausible, naturalistic explanation on the one hand, and a fanciful, incredible one on the other, the evidence for which is based solely on the most undependable evidence: reports by excited eye-witnesses. I think we must choose the former, while realizing that the latter will be preferred by Hollywood producers and others bent on selling a mystery.

References

"Barn Owl." 2001. At www.thebigzoo.com/Animals/Barn_Owl.asp.

Bent, Arthur Cleveland. 1938. *Life Histories of North American Birds of Prey*, part 2; reprinted New York: Dover, 1961, 140–153.

Cerny, Walter. 1975. *A Field Guide in Color to Birds.* London: Cathray Books, 136–137.

Coe, James. 1994. *Eastern Birds: A Guide to Field Identification of North American Species.* New York: Golden Press, 86–87.

Gill, Frank B. 1994. *Ornithology*, 2nd ed. New York: W.H. Freeman and Co., 188.

Keel, John A. 1975. *The Mothman Prophecies.* New York: Signet.

Peterson, Roger Tory. 1957. *How to Know the Birds.* New York: Signet, 85, 100–101.

———, 1980. *Eastern Birds.* New York: Houghton Mifflin, 172–175.

Steward, Laura, ed. 1977. *The Illustrated Encyclopedia of Birds.* London: Octopus Books, 208–209.

"Mothman" Is a Sandhill Crane

Ralph Turner

One night in late 1966, two young couples from Point Pleasant, West Virginia, were terrified when a huge, winged, manlike creature appeared in the light shed by their car headlights. Sightings of the creature, which came to be called Mothman, were reported by many other people over the next several weeks. Then, abruptly, the sightings stopped, and from then on Mothman has only been reported sporadically near Point Pleasant and elsewhere.

During the height of the sightings in late 1966 to early 1967, many townspeople were terrified. Were they and their neighbors seeing some kind of invading extraterrestrial alien, a bizarre and frightening monster, or was there another explanation? Local newspaper reporter Ralph Turner spent at least one night wandering around the creature's favored locale, the abandoned ordnance factory (known as "the TNT area"), but he didn't see the creature himself. He merely got cold and wet and felt rather foolish, he said.

Ralph Turner, "That Mothman: Would You Believe a Sandhill Crane?" *Herald-Dispatch*, November 19, 1966. Copyright © 1966 by the *Herald-Dispatch*. Reproduced by permission.

Turner later interviewed Dr. Robert L. Smith, a forestry assistant professor at the University of West Virginia, to see if there was a scientific explanation for Mothman. The following article is Turner's account of that interview, in which Smith told him that he thought Mothman was most likely a sandhill crane.

The case of the Mason County monster may have been solved Friday [in November 1966] by a West Virginia University professor.

Dr. Robert L. Smith, associate professor of wildlife biology in WVU's division of forestry, told Mason Sheriff George Johnson at Point Pleasant he believes the "thing" which has been frightening people in the Point Pleasant area since Tuesday is a large bird which stopped off while migrating south.

"From all the descriptions I have read about this 'thing' it perfectly matches the sandhill crane," said the professor. "I definitely believe that's what these people are seeing."

Since Tuesday more than 10 people have spotted what they described as a "birdman" or "mothman" in the area of the McClintick Wildlife Station.

They described it as a huge gray-winged creature with large red eyes.

Crane's Similarities to "Mothman"

Dr. Smith said the sandhill crane stands an average of five feet and has gray plumage. A feature of its appearance is a bright red flesh area around each eye. It has an average wing spread of about seven feet.

"Somebody who has never seen anything like it before could easily get the impression it is a flying man," he said.

"Car lights would cause the bare skin to reflect as big red circles around the eyes."

While such birds are rare to this area, Dr. Smith said this is migration time and it would not be too difficult for one or more of the birds to stop off at the wildlife refuge. There are no official sightings of such birds in West Virginia, although there have been unconfirmed reports in the past, he added.

The birds are rarely seen east of the Mississippi now except in Florida. Distribution mainly is in Canada and the population is increasing in the Midwest. They winter in Southern California, in Mexico and along the Gulf Coast.

According to one book, the sandhill crane is a "fit successor" to the great whooping crane which is almost extinct. The book states that the height of the male when it stands erect is nearly that of a man of average stature, while the bird's great wings carry its compact and muscular body with perfect ease at a high speed.

Dr. Smith said that while the birds are powerful fliers they cannot match the 100 mph speed one couple reported the "thing" attained when pursuing their car.

Dr. Smith warned that while the sandhill crane is harmless if left alone, that if cornered it may become a formidable antagonist. Its dagger-like bill is a dangerous weapon which the crane does not hesitate to use when at bay and fighting for its life. Many a hunter's dog has been badly injured, he said.

Eerie Sound

Some of those who reported seeing the "monster" remembered best the eerie sound it made. The description of the sandhill crane also fits there.

"The cry of the sandhill crane is a veritable voice of nature, untamed and unterrified," says one book on birds. "Its uncanny quality is like that of the loon, but is more pronounced because of the much greater volume of the crane's voice. Its resonance is remarkable and its carrying power is increased by a distinct tremolo effect. Often for several minutes after the birds have vanished the unearthly sound drifts back to the listener, like a taunting trumpet from the underworld."

The *"Chupacabras"* May Be a Dog

David Adams

When the *chupacabras* first hit the public consciousness in the fall of 1995, this mysterious livestock-killing animal was a phenomenon relegated almost exclusively to the little island of Puerto Rico. People there reported seeing a small kangaroo-like beast with glowing red eyes and a spiky spine. The creature was said to leap over fences and to kill its prey with a puncture wound to the neck.

Within months of the island's first sightings, *chupacabras* encounters were being reported in Mexico, Central America, and the United States, mostly in Hispanic communities. Something was viciously killing animals, but was it really the weird creature that many witnesses said they saw? Investigators examined what evidence they could find— mainly the wounds on the dead animals and markings on the ground nearby—and some concluded that the killer was really a dog.

In the following article, *St. Petersburg* (Florida) *Times* reporter David Adams describes how the *chupacabras* captured media attention and how investigators came to believe the real culprits were dogs.

When police arrived at the crime scene they had never seen such carnage. Lifeless victims—69 in all—lay strewn across the yards of two families in Sweetwater, a heavily Hispanic neighborhood in south Miami. But it was a Miami massacre with a difference—a case perhaps for Ace Ventura, Pet Detective.

The victims were all animals—goats, chickens, geese and ducks. Who—or what—could have done such a dastardly thing? The killer, say police and a local zoologist, was a large dog. Wrong, say local residents. It was the chupacabras, the Caribbean's very own Bigfoot, except this creature is a vampire-like predator whose name literally means "Goat-sucker" in Spanish. Don't be surprised if you haven't heard of the chupacabras.

Until March 1996 it had never been seen or heard of out-side Puerto Rico, the U.S. island commonwealth of 4-million people. For the past six months, the hideous blood-sucking beast with an oval-head and bulging red-eyes—part reptile, part insect, part UFO alien—allegedly has been ter-rorizing the island's central mountains. But after the slaugh-ter in Sweetwater, the chupacabras has firmly established a place in the annals of Miami make-believe. It may sound like something out of *Star Trek*, but it has gripped more than just the imagination of Hispanic Miami. For those who be-lieve in the chupacabras, the fear is real. In some cases the attack on livestock has caused serious economic loss.

One Sweetwater woman claims to have seen it, and there have been alleged chupacabras attacks in other parts of Mi-ami. The beast has developed a large following in Latino communities across the United States, from New Jersey to California. Authorities are taking the killings seriously—up to a point. A specialist has investigated the deaths, and a county commissioner has called for a police request. "It's mushroomed way out of proportion," says Ron Magill, assistant curator at MetroDade zoo. "I'm sitting here literally in shock."

Big Business

Chupacabras has aroused great interest, and discussion—some of it less than serious—on the Internet, where it has its own home page, complete with sketches created by a Princeton University history student. "This has turned out to be a new kind of folklore," said the student, Hector Armstrong, a native of Puerto Rico. There is even talk of a video-game spinoff, he says. It already has become big business: There are T-shirts, a chupacabras sandwich, live morning radio and a Spanish pop song with a chorus that roughly translated goes like this: "Gotta have fun and party. In case the Goatsucker gonna get me." Last week English-language radio got in on the act when the popular station Y-100 ran a week-long "search of the elusive chupacabras!" offering a $1,000 prize for a real photo of the creature. The station made its own mock effort, sending a reporter into the Sweetwater woods dressed in a goat costume.

The chupacabras coverage was a hit. One of Latin America's most watched Spanish-language TV chat shows, *Cristina*, which is recorded in Miami where it has a large audience, gave credence to the "chupacabras phenomenon" with an hour-long program on it Monday. On the show was Jose "Chemo" Soto, the mayor of Canovanas, a town in Puerto Rico where the chupacabras supposedly has claimed more than 100 victims. Soto, who is running for re-election, offered viewers this grim warning: "Whatever it is, it's highly intelligent. Today it is attacking animals, but tomorrow it may attack people." A former police detective, Soto is known to locals as "Chemo (Indiana) Jones," for his quest to capture the mysterious creature. Using caged goats as bait, Soto leads a weekly monster hunt of local volunteers who patrol the town's surrounding hills—so far to no avail. Also interviewed on *Cristina:* a vet from Puerto Rico—nicknamed Dr. Chupacabras—who claims the wounds he has examined on alleged victims of the beast are "totally abnormal" fang-like punctures. Others on the program included an extraterrestrial philosopher and a writer on UFOs, who believe the chupacabras was sent from another planet to Puerto Rico.

According to Jorge Martin, publisher of *Evidencia,* a magazine on UFO research, aliens are drawn to Puerto Rico by the Arecibo Observatory, the world's largest radio-radar telescope. The killings, whatever their cause, are a serious problem that has frightened many people in Puerto Rico and Miami. This has been fueled by a number of eyewitness accounts from seemingly credible people. At least 15 Canovanas residents claim to have had a close encounter with the monster. "I was looking off the balcony one night, and I saw it step out of a bright light in the back yard," said Michael Negron, a 25-year-old college student. "It was about 3 or 4 feet tall with skin like that of a dinosaur. It had bright red eyes the size of hens' eggs, long fangs and multicolored spikes down its head and back." The creature reportedly disembowelled the family goat, draining the blood from its neck.

Some theories—and eyewitness accounts—are harder to believe than others. Consider the latest sighting in the Puerto Rican town of Caguas, where the chupacabras allegedly entered a bedroom window and mauled a stuffed teddy bear, leaving a "puddle of slime." Critics say the hysteria has been whipped up by sensationalist media that are eager to promote the legend as part of a sales or ratings drive. Puerto Rico is a fertile market for such bizarre tales, due to widespread Afro-Caribbean cultural and religious beliefs that involve animal sacrifices and blood rituals. Officials say folk monster tales are hard to combat with rational explanations.

Classic Canine Evidence

Just ask Magill, the Miami zoologist. When he attended the Sweetwater slaying, he pointed out to residents what he believes to be incontrovertible proof the killer was a large dog, maybe 50 pounds in weight, or more. "They were just totally not listening," he said. On inspection he found the bite marks were "classic canine punctures from dogs." As for the vampire theory, "Contrary to the popular belief, all the animals were full of blood." He demonstrated this on one dead goat. "I took a knife and cut into the carotid artery and blood came out of the carcass." He also showed where he believes a dog dug its way under the garden fence. "It was a classic dog digging. You could see all the dirt pushed back and dog hair on the bottom of the fence." Magill was able to identify footprints as being that of a dog. Residents wanted to know why none of the animals had been eaten. Again he points to what he calls the "classic m.o." of dog attacks. "Dogs don't kill for food, they kill for fun. It's a thrill." For Magill the scene was a deja vu experience. Two years earlier, dogs killed 15 antelopes at the zoo in the same fashion. But Magill says all his explanations were for naught. Local residents were enthralled by heavy media attention that day.

An older woman came out of the house and turning to a group of TV cameras demonstrated how she had confronted the chupacabras. "It stood up on two legs and was hunched over like this with big arms and looked at me with these red eyes," the woman said. "I just said, 'Oh jeez, here we go,'" says a discouraged Magill. "As soon as she did that every news media camera zoomed in on her. That was the footage they played over and over again." Part Cuban, and fluent in Spanish, Magill understands the cultural sensitivity of older people in the Hispanic community over their religious and cultural beliefs. He even believes in UFOs and extraterrestrial life forms. "I'm not one of those pure scientists who say 'No, we are the only ones with the truth and all that stuff is ludicrous,'" he says. "It's just in this case that was not it."

The *Chupacabras* Is a Myth

Robert Friedman

The *chupacabras*, or goatsucker, is said to be a small, vicious creature with kangaroo-like legs, a spiky spine, and red, glowing eyes. Its first widely known appearance was in Puerto Rico in 1995, where it supposedly killed livestock with a puncture wound to the neck and then drained its prey's blood. Despite many reports from people who claim to have seen the *chupacabras*, many experts believe it is a myth. In the following article, *San Juan Star* reporter Robert Friedman discusses some theories about why people believe in the *chupacabras*. He reports that several experts believe that legends of bloodsucking creatures symbolize the fear of poor people that the economic system is sucking away their livelihood and even soul. Others believe that the *chupacabras* phenomenon represents anxiety over epidemics such as AIDS. Some scientists, however, dismiss the belief in *chupacabras* as pure superstition.

The goatsucker is on the go—with new alleged victims reported in [Puerto Rico and] other Caribbean countries, Mexico, Central America and Dade County, Florida. Once strictly *del pais* [of this country, Puerto Rico] the chupacabras, as the supposed vampire-like killer of barnyard animals is known in Spanish, has recently been spotted in the Dominican Republic, Costa Rica, Mexico, and Miami.

The monster—reptilian body, oval head, bulging red eyes, fanged teeth and long, darting tongue—has allegedly pulled off one of the more grisly animal slaughters of late: the one-night massacre of 69 goats, chickens, geese and ducks in the heavily Hispanic Sweetwater neighborhood of South Miami. Miami police and the local zoologist say that the killer was a large dog—but Sweetwater residents insist that the deed was done by the blood-sucking beast first spotted in the central mountains of Puerto Rico [in 1994].

Whatever, the chupacabras phenomenon seems quick becoming part of Hispanic—and possibly international—bestial lore. The goatsucker already has been tagged the Bigfoot of the Caribbean by stateside journalists. The monster made its network TV debut [in April 1996] via *Unsolved Mysteries*. It was the talk of the popular Miami-based gabfest *El Show de Cristina*, which is transmitted throughout Latin America. That show featured Canovanas Mayor Jose "Chemo" Soto, known to townsfolk as "Chemo Jones" for his weekly chupacabra hunts through the surrounding hills, using a caged goat for bait. Soto offered this grim warning: "Whatever it is, it's highly intelligent. Today it is attacking animals, tomorrow it may be attacking people."

Tee shirt sales are said to be booming, a video game reportedly is in the works, songs are sung to Ol' Red Eyes over South Florida radio stations (such as "Chupacabra-fragalisticexpialidotious," as in the song of a similar name from *Mary Poppins*). The beast is on the Internet, courtesy of some Puerto Rican students at Princeton University, who give tongue-in-cheek updates daily on the goat-sucker's doings.

A Recurring Legend

So, what have we here? Among other things, a recurring legend, especially prevalent in Latin America, according to anthropologists, Hispanic historians, and others. "There are a certain number of these legends of bloodsucking animals in South and Latin America," said Richard Grinker, an anthropology professor at George Washington University. "They are usually analyzed as anti-capitalist, an unconscious means of rebellion by country people who believe that capitalism is sucking dry the earth and their entire being." Fellow anthropologist Paul Brodwin acknowledged that blood-sucking legends pre-date quasi-Marxist analyses, but said the legends often get reinterpreted "according to social circumstances."

Take, for instance, the legend of the Loup Garou, which Brodwin has studied in the Haitian countryside. This some-time human–sometime animal being is related to the French werewolf legend, said Brodwin. But with a difference. The Loup Garou sucks the blood of its human victims. The Haitian legend has been analyzed as a "collective fantasy," said the University of Wisconsin–Milwaukee professor, of an unconscious suspicion and fear the poorer-than-poor have of their neighbors.

Marvette Perez, curator of Hispanic history at the Smithsonian Institution's American History Museum, sees deja vu once more in the chupacabras tales. Perez, a native of Arecibo [Puerto Rico], recalled the similarities between the chupacabras and both the Moca vampire and the garadiablo of island lore. A couple of decades ago, the Moca monster was sucking blood of assorted animals around that small mountain town, while the garadiablo was a devilish looking creepy crawly from the lagoon seen in local swamplands. "This seems to be a very Caribbean phenomenon, especially of the Spanish-speaking islands," said Perez. "It's part of our folklore. It's interesting that the chupacabras has not been found on the English-speaking islands, but has migrated only in places where people speak Spanish."

Vampire Tales

Pedro Vidal, professor of Spanish and Latin American Studies at American University, remembers hearing childhood tales in his native Venezuela of a beast sucking the blood not only of animals, but also of little children. Vidal, who has done research on vampires, noted that the hemispheric roots of such entities go way back, to the Mayans, who worshipped a "vampire figure deity long before the idea of Dracula."

Bram Stoker's novel of the blood-thirsty count became a big hit in Victorian England in an age of anxiety over a syphilis epidemic, said Vidal. Now, another sexually transmitted epidemic has unsettled the populace. Puerto Rico, he noted, is among the areas in the hemisphere hardest hit by AIDS. It is entirely possible, he said, that the commotion over the chupacabras could be linked to the AIDS fear.

Unbeknownst to many, there is a real live goatsucker in captivity in the Washington, D.C. zoo. In fact, ornithologists know all about goatsuckers—which is the name given to a family of nocturnal birds. They are described as soft-feathered with long, pointed wings, short, weak legs and feet, a very small bill, but a wide, gaping mouth, and whose eyes reflect light at night. Some goatsuckers of note are night jars, whippoorwills and the Australian frog mouth, which is on display at the D.C. zoo. Could they be . . . ? Most unlikely, said Bob Hoage of National Zoo. The winged goat-suckers feed almost exclusively on insects, he noted.

The goatsucker tag comes from the Latin word *Caprimul-gus*. The birds are often found in the Mediterranean in places where goats graze. In a strange twist, bird-watcher-columnist Don Wilson reports in the *Orlando Sun Sentinel* that "the harmless whippoorwill was once viewed as a sinister creature. Superstitious country folk once believed the birds sucked the milk from goats' udders, causing them to dry up."

The Modern Pterodactyl Photo Is a Hoax

Massimo Polidoro

When people argue that pterodactyls or their relatives still exist in the modern world, they sometimes point to the evidence provided by a famous photograph purporting to show a pterodactyl-like bird killed by Arizona cowboys around 1890. The photo supposedly appeared in a magazine in the 1950s, and a few parapsychologists claim that they remember seeing it. However, several researchers in recent times have scoured all kinds of archives and have been unable to find the photo. Although that photo, if it ever existed, appears to be permanently lost, a similar photo can be found on the Internet today. It purports to show Civil War soldiers with a dead pterodactyl. Many Internet users believe it is proof that pterodactyls did—and still might—coexist with humans. Since most scientists believe pterodactyls are long extinct, proof of their current existence would be big news indeed.

Massimo Polidoro, "Notes on a Strange World: A Pterodactyl in the Civil War," *Skeptical Inquirer*, May/June 2002, pp. 21–23. Copyright © 2002 by the Committee for the Scientific Investigation of Claims of the Paranormal. Reproduced by permission.

However, Massimo Polidoro asserts in the following article that the Civil War photograph is definitely a fake. He provides evidence that it originated on a website for a fictional television program about the paranormal, and he is dismayed that the photo was co-opted from the website and is currently circulating the Internet as supposed evidence of a historical anomaly. Polidoro and others argue that the rumored western cowboy photo, if it actually existed, was a fake as well. Polidoro believes there is no evidence that pterodactyls have existed anywhere since the end of the dinosaur age.

Polidoro is a stage magician, an investigator of the paranormal, the author of several Italian books on the paranormal, and the head of Comitato Italiano per il Controllo delle Affermazioni sul Paranormale (CICAP), an Italian skeptics organization.

Most people know about the plot of *Jurassic Park*, the Steven Spielberg movie inspired by the Michael Crichton bestseller: dinosaurs are brought back to life thanks to the wonders of genetic engineering. The dinosaurs were so real that the movie instantly became a huge success. It was obvious that a new Crichton book and subsequent Spielberg movie, *The Lost World*, would be produced. Again a fantastic success and more sequels to come (though with Crichton and Spielberg still more or less involved, but not in the limelight anymore).

Lost World

Not many, however, know that the original idea for dinosaurs still living in the modern era and interacting with humans dates back to 1912 when Arthur Conan Doyle, then already a worldwide celebrity thanks to the adventures of his cool private detective Sherlock Holmes, published one of his most famous novels, *The Lost World.* It was not a coincidence—nor a theft—but a tribute to the old master, then, that Crichton would give the same title to his own book.

In Doyle's book, a group of explorers, led by the energetic Professor Challenger, sets sail for a lost land in South America (a place where Crichton would stage his stories as well) and discovers that dinosaurs, long believed to be extinct, still live. The group survives a million adventures and then is able to make it back to London. At a public lecture at Queen's Hall they try to convince a skeptical audience of the wonders they witnessed but words, drawings, and fuzzy pictures are not enough. The only thing that could have an effect would be the presence of a real creature.

And the creature is there: "[A] large square packing-case was slowly carried forward and placed in front of the Professor's chair. All sound had hushed in the audience and everyone was absorbed in the spectacle before them. Professor Challenger drew off the top of the case, which formed a sliding lid. Peering down into the box he snapped his fingers several times and was heard from the Press seat to say, 'Come, then, pretty, pretty!' in a coaxing voice. An instant later, with a scratching, rattling sound, a most horrible and loathsome creature appeared from below and perched itself upon the side of the case. The face of the creature was like the wildest gargoyle that the imagination of a mad medieval builder could have conceived. It was malicious, horrible, with two small red eyes as bright as points of burning coal. Its long, savage mouth, which was held half-open, was full of a double row of sharklike teeth. Its shoulders were humped, and round them were draped what appeared to be a faded gray shawl. It was the devil of our childhood in person."

Lost Creatures

That's the description of a pterodactyl, the ancient prehistoric winged reptile that lived between 144 and 65 million years ago. When Doyle wrote his book, dinosaurs and pterodactyls were of course long gone. Imagine how fantastic it would be if, somewhere, somehow, some dinosaur were still alive; that's exactly what many believe the Loch Ness or the Ogopogo "monsters" are, or what other mysterious creatures could be. Animals that lived when dinosaurs roamed are still with us and will probably still be here for a long time, such as sharks, crocodiles, and turtles, for example.

Yes, you'd say, but there's a huge difference between a lone, mysterious, gigantic creature that is said to live in a lake—but of which nobody seems to be able to take a decent picture—and animals that any school kid can meet at an aquarium. Okay, one could answer, but what do you say about the fact that prehistoric creatures that were thought to be extinct are still found to be alive? That's what happened with the coelacanth, for example, of which a living specimen was discovered only in 1952. And, surprisingly, "new" animals can still be found in our small world: animals such as the okapi, the Komodo dragon, the mountain gorilla, the Manchurian brown bear, or the giant panda, were all discovered only in the twentieth century. Even to this day, huge and unexpected new creatures can be found: What would you call, in fact, the chance filming by an underwater expedition in May 2001 of a big, strange-looking, and never-seen-before squid (more than seventeen feet long)?

Now, you'd probably admit that the possibility of finding an unexpected "dinosaur," or at least some creature that lived millions of years ago, appears to be more plausible. But, would you be ready to stretch your willingness to the point of imagining a real, living pterodactyl, flying through North America? Some people did.

Lost Picture

It all began in April 26, 1890, when the *Tombstone Epitaph*, an Arizona local newspaper, published a sensational story: "Found in the Desert—A Strange Winged Monster Discovered And Killed On The Huachuca Desert." In it the monster was described as "a huge alligator with an extremely elongated tail and an immense pair of wings." The monster had been sighted and shot by two ranchers who were returning home from the Huachuca Desert. When the creature was certainly dead, they proceeded to make an examination and "found that it measured about ninety-two feet in length and the greatest diameter was about fifty inches." The wingspan, "from tip to tip," was about 160 feet. The wings, as in the pterodactyl, were "composed of a thick and nearly transparent membrane and were devoid of feathers or hair, as was the entire body."

Unfortunately, according to the story, the two cowboys left the monster where it was and only cut off a small portion of the tip of one wing as a souvenir. A search, however, was to be sent next day "for examination by the eminent scientists of the day." No trace of the bird or of the commission's report, however, has ever appeared. Harry McClure, a youngster early last century in Lordsburg, New Mexico, when the two ranchers came to town, remembered the episode. He had friends who knew them well and thought the story was not a hoax. Was the creature photographed? No, it was not, according to McClure, and in any case the *Epitaph* did not carry any pictures with its article.

Others, however, think differently. Writer Jack Pearl told about the *Epitaph* story in a 1963 issue of *Saga Magazine* and explained that the strange bird was brought to town and photographed. It was put in a wagon and, after reaching Tombstone, was nailed to the wall of a barn: six men stood before it with their arms outstretched touching fingertip to fingertip. Pearl, however, seems to have gotten many details wrong, as Mark Hall clearly explained in *Fortean Times* magazine, and the story of the picture has never received any corroboration. There were many, though, who remembered seeing such a photograph, or a photocopy of it, in the hands of Ivan T. Sanderson, the famous naturalist and *Fortean* author who died in 1973. Apparently, Sanderson gave the photocopy to two young men who travelled into the heart of northern Pennsylvania to inquire about reports of giant birds in that region and lost it in the course of their search. All kinds of publications were searched, from *National Geographic* to *Fate* magazine, including all the back issues of the *Epitaph*, but no traces of such a photo were ever found.

"The numerous vague recollections of seeing this missing photograph," concludes Hall in his article, "might well be erroneous. Like many others, I have spent many hours looking for it and like them I will continue to look. Everyone who reads about this phantom photograph has the same desire to see it for themselves." And then, after many years, a mysterious picture emerges from the Internet.

Lost Chance

In the spring of 2000 a new Web site (www.freakylinks.com) appeared and published a sensational photograph showing a group of what appeared to be Union soldiers before the carcass of a massive pterodactyl! The editor of the site, Derek Barnes, claimed that the photo was found in July of 1998 "squeezed between the pages of a 70's cheesy paranormal book bought at a thrift store." The photograph, sepia tinted, scratched, bent, and torn on the edges, appeared to be very impressive and, apparently, its authenticity was verified by various experts. One historian had identified the men's uniforms as "typical of Union Volunteers around 1861–1862." Another expert, an "M. Nance Darbrow, professor of paleontology from the University of Florida," asserted that no one at that time could have known about pterodactyls, as the first fossils were not discovered in North America until 1871. "This photograph," commented Barnes in his Web pages, "is either going to be the biggest paranormal news scoop of the century or it's going to make me the biggest fool on the planet. Or perhaps both."

Was, then, the holy grail of cryptozoology located at last? Alright, it did not have the cowboys standing before the bird but civil war soldiers instead. Was it perhaps a different pterodactyl? *Fortean Times* ran a very skeptical article about this photo in its May 2000 issue, concluding with these words: "We believe he's a hoaxer but a clever and well-informed one as the site is full of excellent fortean jokes— e.g., the rather disgusting photo of a toilet bowl thoughtfully snapped after some unfortunate had just vomited frogs."

Further doubts soon emerged after the magazine's article was published. Various readers wrote to pinpoint several details in the photo that led to the conclusion that the photo was a fake. First of all, the men pictured were obviously re-enactors, "given the undue proportion of over-age and over-weight members in their ranks—the average Civil War soldier was a scrawny youth of nineteen." Such groups of re-enactors are quite common in the States and, among them "there is a much higher proportion of older and fatter members than in the original armies." The clean and neat uniforms "also mark them out as re-enactors rather than the real thing." Their poses, also, are "too naturalistic for an 1860s photograph"; if you've ever looked at photos from that period "you can see there are a dozen subtle differences in the way they stood, the way they held their heads, the looks on their faces, and what they did with their arms and hands while they were being photographed."

Finally, all doubts were confirmed when it was discovered that the site was connected to the creators of *The Blair Witch Project*. *FreakyLinks* was in fact the title of an upcoming TV series, and the site was designed to promote interest in it. The show star was actor Ethan Embry and his character was named "Derek Barnes, Editor of an Internet Web site that investigates the paranormal." As expected, the experts quoted in the site were imaginary, just as the pterodactyl that was only a stage prop courtesy of Fox. The cryptozoologists' hope of having finally found real proof of a living pterodactyl in the modern era, then, returned to the world of dreams. But if somewhere an unknown magazine or book truly contains an old picture of a mysterious bird, it will hopefully be found some day.

References

Anonymous, 1980. Found in the desert. *Tombstone Epitaph*, 26 April.

Anonymous, 2000. Is this a pterodactyl? *Fortean Times* May: 21.

Barnes, Dere, 2000. How many pterodactyls did you kill in the war, daddy? www.freakylinks.com.

Crichton, Michael, 1990. *Jurassic Park*. New York: Alfred A. Knopf, Inc.

———, 1995. *The Lost World*. New York: Alfred A. Knopf, Inc.

Doyle, Arthur Conan, 1912. *The Lost World*. London: Hodder and Stoughton.

Hall, Mark, 1997. Thunderbirds are go. *Fortean Times* December: 34–38.

Letters, 2000. Pterodactyl photo. *Fortean Times* August: 52.

McClure, Harry F., 1970. Tombston's flying monster. *Old West Magazine* Summer. 6(4): 2.

Pearl, Jack, 1964. Monster bird that carries off people. *Saga Magazine* May: 29–31, 83–85.

Vecchione, M., et al., 2001. Worldwide observations of remarkable deep-sea squids. *Science* 294: 2505, December 21.

Giant Birds Are Not Remnants of the Dinosaur Age

Karl P.N. Shuker

Numerous people in different parts of the world have reported seeing gigantic birds that do not seem to belong to the typical bird species in their areas. Often, witnesses are convinced that these birds are pterodactyls, which scientists say died out with the dinosaurs. Karl P.N. Shuker, author of the following article, argues that the giant bird sightings can be explained by known bird species. The article briefly describes several sightings and Shuker's belief about what witnesses actually saw.

Shuker is a zoologist who has studied ordinary and not-so-ordinary animals for the past twenty years. He's the author of several books, including *Dragons: A Natural History* and *In Search of Prehistoric Survivors: Do Giant "Extinct" Creatures Still Exist?*

Many cryptozoological publications have included eye-witness accounts of mysterious winged dragon-like beasts reported from Africa and the U.S.A. that resemble living representatives of those familiar flying reptiles from prehistory known as pterosaurs, typified by the pterodactyls. Less well known, however, is that these creatures' files also contain several reports emanating from far beyond those geographical confines.

J. Richard Greenwell, secretary of the International Society of Cryptozoology, has a Mexican correspondent who claims that there are living pterosaurs in eastern Mexico and is determined to capture one, to prove beyond any shadow of a doubt that they do exist. Worthy of note is that certain depictions of deities, demons, and strange beasts from ancient Mexican mythology are decidedly pterodactylian in appearance. One particularly intriguing example is the mysterious "serpent-bird" portrayed in relief sculpture amid the Mayan ruins of Tajin, in Veracruz's northeastern portion, noted in 1968 by visiting Mexican archaeologist Dr. José Diaz-Bolio, and dating from a mere 1,000 to 5,000 years ago. Yet all pterosaurs had officially become extinct at least sixty-four million years ago. So how do we explain the Mayan serpent-bird—a non-existent, imaginary beast, or a creature lingering long after its formal date of demise? Although neither solution would be unprecedented, only one is correct. But which one?

Around February 1947, J. Harrison from Liverpool was on a boat navigating an estuary of the Amazon river when he and some others aboard spied a flock of five huge birds flying overhead in "V" formation, with long necks and beaks, and each with a wingspan of about twelve feet. According to Harrison, however, their wings resembled brown leather and appeared to be featherless. As they soared down the river, he could see that their heads were flat on top, and the wings seemed to be ribbed. Judging from the sketch that he prepared, however, they bore little resemblance to pterosaurs, and were far more reminiscent of a large stork, three of which, the jabiru, maguari, and wood ibis, are native here.

New Zealand "Pterodactyl"

A bird is also more likely than a pterosaur to be the explanation for the blue-winged red "pterodactyl" spied flying with an undulating motion over a new motorway in New Zealand sometime prior to 1982. If such a conspicuously colored beast was markedly pterosaurian in appearance, there would surely have been other sightings on record, but none has so far been brought to cryptozoological attention.

One morning in July 1987 or thereabouts, near a small river in Crete's Asteroussia Mountains, three youngsters allegedly spied what looked at first like a giant dark gray bird flying low towards the mountains. As it approached them, however, they could see that its wings were membranous, like those of a bat, with finger-like projections. It also had a pelican-like beak and clawed feet. After poring through several books, they learned that the animal bearing the closest resemblance to their mystery beast was the pterodactyl.

Last and least is the infamous French pterodactyl that supposedly emerged, weak but nonetheless alive, from out of a hollow boulder blasted apart during the excavation of a new railway tunnel at Culmout, according to an *Illustrated London News* report for February 9, 1856. As soon as it took its first breath of air, however, it promptly expired. Here, therefore, was a true prehistoric survivor—not a modern-day descendant of an ancient line, but a bona fide prehis-

toric creature that had somehow survived in suspended an-
imation for more than sixty-four million years. When its
body was examined by an anonymous expert, he was able
to identify its species very precisely—*Pterodactylus anas*. Yet,
amazingly, nothing more was ever heard of this zoologically
priceless specimen.

No Such Species

In reality, of course, there is no such species, and there was
no such specimen either, but none of this should come as
any surprise to the linguistically minded, for whom all of
the clues for deciphering the true nature of this tall tale are
readily available. After all, "anas" is Latin for "duck," which
in French (the pterodactyl was found in France) is *canard*—
a word with a very different meaning in English [a false
report]!

The "Dover Demon" Likely Was a Moose

Martin S. Kottmeyer

When experienced investigators examine cases involving mysterious monsters, they often find that there is a simple explanation: Witnesses have simply mistaken something ordinary for something extraordinary. A trick of light and shadows makes one thing look like something else. A misjudgment of distance makes something appear to be gigantic when it really is not. Was the Dover Demon such a case?

The Dover Demon is a puzzling creature that appeared in only one place—Dover, Massachusetts—during one weekend in 1977, but it remains a part of the area's mysterious lore. The Dover Demon was reported by credible witnesses to be a big-headed, red-eyed beast of unfamiliar form. The witnesses were sure they had seen a monster, but had they? Martin S. Kottmeyer thinks they may have seen something much more ordinary: a baby moose. In the following article, he examines the witnesses' accounts to see if they could fit such a prosaic explanation.

Martin S. Kottmeyer, "Demon Moose," *The Anomalist*, Spring 1998, pp. 104–10. Copyright © 1998 by *The Anomalist*. Reproduced by permission.

Kottmeyer is an investigator of paranormal phenomena and the author of many articles on paranormal topics.

Something mysterious and disturbing happened in Dover, Massachusetts in April 1977. Over a period of two nights, four people in three locations saw a smallish beast with a peculiar head shaped more or less like a watermelon. Bill Bartlett, the first witness, said it had eyes that glowed a bright orange. His sketch showed a creature standing on four spindly limbs that each ended in long fingers that splayed over some rocks it seemed posed on. It had a slender torso and a neck that looked inadequate to the task of holding that long head.

It acquired the catchy tag "The Dover Demon."[1] This was presumably inspired by the glowing eyes. The creature, neither in Bartlett's encounter nor the subsequent sightings by John Baxter, Abby Brabham and Will Taintor, ever did anything remotely malevolent beyond simply existing. It didn't abduct anyone or perform nasty things on anyone's body. Basically it just stood, moved a little, and then it wasn't being seen. Curiously its defining trait—the eyes—is the object of the most blatant contradictions among the witnesses. Baxter did not remark on the eyes glowing at all. Abby Brabham maintained the eyes glowed bright green in contrast to Bartlett's orange, even upon being "questioned closely" by investigators on the point. The larger problem with the tag is that, in devil-lore, the Devil's eyes typically glowed red.

Still, if it wasn't a demon, what was it? . . .

An Unknown Earthly Animal?

All four witnesses thought what they saw was an unknown terrestrial animal that had previously gone undetected in

Dover's dense woods. A neighbor suggested it was a fox dis-
figured by a disease which makes foxes swell up and lose
hair. Comments by witnesses that it was the size of a monkey apparently led to thoughts that the Dover Demon was
an escaped lab animal. Nobody came forward to identify it,
however. The drawings and descriptions are correctly used
to dismiss these ideas. Most people familiar with the kids
felt they "saw something." The father of the Taintor teen
had the sense that it was a conventional animal of some
sort, but it somehow got mistaken for the demon.

Though awkwardly expressed, I think he had the right
idea. I got the impression from the testimony that there was
probably a real animal at the root of things, but it was seen
briefly or in poor circumstances that didn't give enough vi-
sual detail to form a proper gestalt and give a firm identification. Investigators determined Bartlett saw it in headlights
for only five or six seconds. Brabham and Taintor were driving past it and caught a glimpse in the headlights for maybe
five seconds. Baxter saw it for a matter of minutes, but he
was walking in darkness and the optimal moment of observation consisted of a silhouette against an open field.

Bartlett's drawing seems bizarre at first consideration, but
the basic body plan is not unusual; four limbs, a torso, a
neck, a head, and two eyes. It is fundamentally the shape of
the head and the unfamiliar proportions of the various elements that prove most confusing. My attention eventually
focused on the long head and thin legs as leading the way
to an unconsidered alternative explanation. It faintly reminded me of a moose. The small size and absence of horns
would mean it had to be quite young, perhaps a yearling recently weened in advance of the mother giving an April
birth. Dig out the wildlife guides and test out the details.

A moose calf has legs relatively longer than the adult. Its
coat is light-colored with a dark muzzle and marks over the

eyes. It lacks a shoulder hump. Moose live only in densely forested areas, usually near shallow lakes or swamps. They have short necks and tend to graze on shrubs and trees. If a tree is small, they may straddle it with their front legs and try to break it down. They are particularly fond of the upper bark of aspens. They also like ground juniper, a type of yew called "shintangle." They have no fear of the ooze of swamps and will swim in lakes to feed on water lilies and other water growing plants. Their range in the U.S. includes all of New England down to Pennsylvania.[2]

Supporting Details

Bartlett's placing of the eyes matches the placement of eyes just above the hip of the muzzle on a moose's head. The lack of a discernable nose and mouth is easily laid to the fact that nostrils and mouth are very far down on the muzzle. A drawing of a young moose presents the ears swept back along the line of the head and would not discernably stick out, thus accounting for the absence of visible ears.

The skin was described as hairless with something like dirt smudged on it and appeared to be the rough texture of a shark. My guess is it had emerged from a nearby lake and was still wet. Bartlett and Brabham "believed it must be a water creature of some kind since it was seen not far from water in all three instances." Bartlett said it was a peach color. Brabham and Taintor said it was beige or tan. This is roughly consistent with the lighter reddish-brown coat of young moose. Bartlett also said the tint was lighter, almost whitish, near the hands. This is true of moose legs generally, Brabham and Taintor said the facial area around the eyes were lighter. This could be the marks over the eyes of the young mentioned in the guide. Finally, Bartlett and Brabham and Taintor commented on the possible absence of a tail, though by their own admission the angle might have hid it. Moose have tails that are short and flat and lay against the haunches in a manner that would probably render them too indistinct to be noticed at first glance.

The most blatant objection will be the long fingers at the bottom of the limbs on Bartlett's drawing. They obviously aren't standard equipment on moose. Indeed, there are not any animals with such long fingers on both front and back pairs of limbs which come to mind. Bipeds aren't built like that, let alone quadrapeds. My thought is that these may be vines caught in the hooves, torn, and dragged in lake mud. Baxter spoke of the fingers being "molded around the top of a rock" during his sighting, and this seems more suggestive of wet vegetation than articulated appendages.

Against this, Baxter's drawing shows fingers wrapped around a tree. The proximity to a tree hints at moose feeding habits and it might be attempting a straddling posture to either reach leaves or bend the tree down. It also invites reflection about the humanoid solution. Do aliens eat trees? Do they like to hug trees? There seems to be no precedent for such behavior in the UFO literature either prior to or subsequent to this case. It seems puzzlingly unique. It could be the wrapping of the fingers was an interpolated detail arising from a vague sense of what the creature was doing in the dark.

Glowing Eyes

A last problem that should be addressed are the glowing eyes. The glow was evidently eyeshine associated with automobile headlights. Bartlett and Brabham and Taintor were using cars and saw it; Baxter who was walking did not. The fact that Bartlett reported orange eyeshine and Brabham a bright green is not a serious objection against the case. Personal experience and experiments with cattle have proven to me that one can get a range of colors in eyeshine spreading from orange to yellow to bright blue-green, even in a given individual animal. The color changes with movement of either the head or the light source to different angles. Typically both eyes change together, though at unusual angles one can get different shades of eyeshine from the two eyes separately. Could the same be true of moose?

In *The Deer of North America*, Leonard Lee Rue III states that deer also display a range of color in their eyeshine, spanning red, orange, yellow, and green.[3] The eye acts as a prism as the light hits the cones of the eyes and bounces back through the retina. As moose are considered as belonging to the same zoological family as deer (i.e. cervidae), the same principle doubtless applies. Data specifically on eyeshine in moose proved too obscure to locate.

I don't consider this solution as having full certitude and I hope this need not be emphasized. I assert only that this solution is better than the alternatives. . . . I think a moose makes a better explanation of the details of the report and avoids the inevitable problems of invoking supernatural entities. Even good mysteries can have prosaic solutions.

Notes

1. Loren Coleman, *Mysterious America*, Faber & Faber, 1983, p. 41.
2. Bernard Grzimek (ed.), *Grzimek's Animal Life Encyclopedia*, Van Nostrand Reinhold Co., 1972, pp. 230–8; *Audubon Nature Encyclopedia*, National Audubon Society, 1965, pp. 1203–7.
3. Leonard Lee Rue III, *The Deer of North America*, Grolier Book Clubs, 1989, pp. 199–200.

Epilogue: Analyzing the Evidence

E very year hundreds of mysterious monster sightings occur around the world. Here is a small sampling of the strange creatures reported recently: In January 2002 huge black creatures, seven feet long and three feet wide, were repeatedly sighted in the Tikis River in the Philippines; in September 2002 huge maned cats, estimated to weigh between six hundred and eight hundred pounds, were reported in Arkansas and Tennessee; in April 2003 a bizarre catlike animal was caught exsanguinating (draining the blood of) chickens in Argentina; in May 2003 a half-man, half-horse creature was said to be terrorizing the people of Maru, Nigeria; also in May, a Vermont woman reportedly saw Memphre, a creature similar to a plesiosaur that supposedly lives in Lake Memphremagog, located near Newport City, Vermont. The question is, how many of these sightings are actually of mysterious monsters and how many of them can be explained in other ways.

When considering a controversial topic like mysterious monsters, it is important to look carefully at the available evidence from more than one point of view. You can begin to shape your beliefs by critically examining the evidence provided by experts who have studied mysterious monsters or investigated alleged monster sightings as well as the evidence from those who claim to have seen, smelled, heard, or been terrorized by one. Each article in this book provides various kinds of evidence and makes various kinds of arguments favoring or challenging the reality of such creatures. Some articles directly contradict others. It is the reader's job to decide which articles present a truthful and reasonable case.

You can do this by reading each article critically. This does not mean that you criticize, or say negative things about, an article. It means that you analyze and evaluate what the author says. This chapter describes a critical reading technique and provides practice using it to evaluate the articles in this book. You can use the same technique to evaluate information about other topics.

The Author

In deciding whether an article provides good evidence for or against the existence of mysterious monsters, it can be helpful to find out something about the author. Consider whether the author has any special qualifications for writing about the subject or any known biases toward it. For example, in this book some authors describe their personal encounters with a mysterious monster. Others are experienced investigators or scientists. You will have to decide what kind of qualifications makes an author more credible.

In this book, the editor has provided at least a small amount of information about each author. Use this information to start forming your opinion about the author's claims.

Hypothetical Reasoning

Despite whether you know anything about the author, you can evaluate an article on its own merits by using hypothetical reasoning. This is a method for determining whether something makes sense—whether an author has made a reasonable case for his or her claims. For example, Linda Scarberry claims that she and her friends actually encountered a mysterious winged man called Mothman. You can use hypothetical reasoning to decide whether she has made a reasonable case supporting her claim. (Keep in mind that hypothetical reasoning will not necessarily prove that an author's claims are true—only that he or she has made a reasonable case for the claims. By determining this, you know whether the argument is worth considering when you are deciding whether mysterious monsters are real.)

To use hypothetical reasoning to analyze an article, you will use five steps:

- State the author's claim (the hypothesis).
- Gather the author's evidence supporting the claim.
- Examine the author's evidence.
- Consider alternative hypotheses, or explanations, for the evidence.
- Draw a conclusion about the author's claim.

Using hypothetical reasoning to examine several articles on mysterious monsters—or on a particular monster—can give you a better perspective on the topic. You will begin to discern the difference between strong and weak evidence and to see which point of view has the most—or the best—evidence supporting it.

The following sections show how to use hypothetical reasoning to critically examine some of the articles in this book. You can practice applying the method to other articles.

1. State the Author's Claim

A hypothesis is a factual statement that can be tested to determine the likelihood of its truth. In other words, it is not merely someone's opinion: By testing it, you can find out if it is likely to be true or false. To evaluate an article critically, start by stating the author's claim. This will be the hypothesis you are going to test as you critically examine the article. The author may make several claims. To simplify, the following table states only one claim for each article.

One important thing to remember when you write a hypothesis is that it should be a factual statement that is clear,

Author	Hypothesis
Linda Scarberry	We saw a mysterious monster called Mothman.
John A. Keel	Mothman is a paranormal creature.
Bucky McMahon	
Jorge Martin	The *chupacabras* is a mysterious monster.
David Hatcher Childress	Remnants of the dinosaur age still fly our skies.
Jerome Clark and Loren Coleman	
Joe Nickell	What people call Mothman is really a common barn owl.
Ralph Turner	
David Adams	People have mistaken dogs for a *chupacabras*.
Robert Friedman	People blame the mythical *chupacabras* for modern problems.
Massimo Polidoro	
Karl P.N. Shuker	"Mysterious" giant birds are really ordinary creatures.
Martin S. Kottmeyer	The "Dover Demon" was simply a misperceived baby moose.

specific, and provable as true or false. Look at the hypothesis stated for the Jorge Martin article. It is vague: How does one define "mysterious monster"? A better hypothesis is "the *chupacabras* looks like a predatory kangaroo" or "*chupacabras* always shows up after there have been UFO sightings." Both of these statements are more specific than the original hypothesis, and they are provable, the first by looking at eyewitness accounts and the second by comparing *chupacabras* reports with UFO reports.

Be aware that not every article has a provable hypothesis.

If an article is purely a writer's opinion, you may not be able to state a provable hypothesis. Likewise, some authors avoid stating any clear claim. For example, many newspaper and magazine article writers attempt to remain as objective as possible about a topic. They simply report what happened and what people said about it. You may not be able to write a provable hypothesis for such an article.

In the table above, several hypothesis spaces have been left empty. Write a clear, specific, and provable hypothesis for each of these articles.

2. Gather the Author's Evidence Supporting the Claim

Once you have a hypothesis, you must gather the evidence the author uses to support that hypothesis. The evidence is everything the author uses to prove that his or her claim is true. Sometimes an individual sentence is a piece of evidence. Sometimes a string of paragraphs or a section of the article is a piece of evidence. Let's look at the article by Jorge Martin, "The *Chupacabras* Is No Ordinary Predator." Here is some of the evidence Martin presents:

1. Martin states that a "weird creature" has killed thousands of animals in Puerto Rico.
2. The dead animals have been found with small, perfectly circular holes in their necks and with their blood drained.
3. Carlos Santos, "a qualified veterinary," has said that the wounds appear to have been inflicted with premeditation and intelligence.
4. The nature of the puncture wounds, without any corresponding wounds on the opposite side of the neck, suggests that "no ordinary animal" inflicted them.
5. Government officials have refused to reveal all of their data about the *chupacabras*.

6. Witness reports describe a strange creature, "a cross between . . . a 'Grey' alien humanoid . . . and . . . the body of a bipedal, erect dinosaur, but with no tail."

7. Madeline Tolentino and her neighbors saw the creature walking down the street in broad daylight.

8. At least two of these creatures have been captured by government officers.

9. UFOs have been sighted in the same areas where the mutilated animals have been found.

10. A Chinese-Russian scientist has produced genetically manipulated species of "electronically-crossed plant and animal organisms."

11. The U.S. government has conducted many secret experiments on Puerto Ricans, including some that caused birth defects. This implies that the *chupacabras* may be a result of secret experiments also.

12. Blood samples do not match those of any known Earth animal.

3. Examine the Evidence the Author Uses to Support the Claim

An author might use many types of evidence to support his or her claims. It is important to recognize different types of evidence and to evaluate whether they actually support the author's claims. Evidence in the list above includes statements of fact (items 1, 2, 8, 9, 10, and 11), logical reasoning (item 5), expert testimony (item 3), physical evidence (items 2, 4, and 12), and eyewitness testimony (items 6, 7, and 9).

Statements of fact (items 1, 2, 8, 9, 10, and 11). A statement of fact presents verifiable information—that is, it can be proven to be true or false. Either the author verifies the information by providing the source of the information or the reader researches and determines whether the statement is true. Ideally, the author should provide the source of any statement of fact so that the reader can confirm it. However, many authors simply expect the reader to take their word for it. Be careful about accepting facts just because an author states them.

In Martin's article, he makes many statements of fact without providing a way for the reader to verify them. For example, Martin does not give us any information about how he knows that the deaths of thousands of animals have been attributed to the *chupacabras*. We might be able to discover this information if we search through many newspapers from Puerto Rico, but we might not.

The reader must decide how important the author's statements of fact are in proving that the hypothesis is true. Considering items 1, 2, 8, 9, 10, and 11, which ones best support the hypothesis that the *chupacabras* is different from any known animal? Which ones do not support the hypothesis?

Logical reasoning (item 5). Authors often use examples of logical reasoning to lead the reader to the author's desired conclusion. Here is an example: A strange creature was seen crouching over a dead goat. The goat had unusual bite wounds. Therefore, the strange creature probably killed the goat. This seems pretty logical. The danger is that sometimes what seems logical really is not. This is called a logical fallacy. Here is an example: I have never seen a *chupacabras:* therefore, the *chupacabras* does not exist. This is a fallacy because it is an overgeneralization. There are a lot of things you have not experienced that are real. For example, you have not experienced spaceflight, the bubonic plague, or death, yet all exist.

Another kind of logical fallacy is a false analogy—you wrongly compare two things based on a common quality. Here is an example: Dogs wag their tails when they are happy; cats that wag their tails must be happy, too. The fallacy is assuming that cats have the same behavior as dogs even though they are a different species. A cat wagging its tail may be angry, indecisive, or ready to pounce on prey. Cats do not typically wag their tails when they are happy.

Sometimes an author does not spell out the logical reasoning. He or she provides part of the reasoning and leaves the reader to assume the rest. This is called *implied logical reasoning*. For example, in item 5 the author wants the reader to assume that since the government has not revealed all of its data about the *chupacabras*, the government is hiding something important, and, in all likelihood, sinister— perhaps that this mysterious monster is related to UFOs or to secret government experiments.

Just as with fully spelled out logical reasoning, if an author uses implied logical reasoning, the reader must decide whether it makes sense. Does item 5 use logical reasoning, or is it a logical fallacy? Why?

Expert or celebrity testimonial (item 3). Many writers support their hypotheses with testimony from a celebrity or an expert. An easy way to understand the use of celebrity or expert testimonial is to look at television ads. A lot of them use this persuasive technique. For example, you have probably seen pop stars and famous athletes in commercials selling cars, shoes, cell phones, and food products, and you likely have seen medicine commercials in which doctors describe the benefits of a product. Advertisers know that many people are influenced when a celebrity or expert says something is true. Article writers know this as well.

Keep in mind that celebrity testimony usually does not have much value as evidence: If a celebrity likes a certain brand of shoes, does it mean the shoes are comfortable and will wear well? Not necessarily. What it really means is that the celebrity's agent got the celebrity a certain amount of money to say the shoes are good.

However, some expert testimony can serve as valuable evidence. For example, in an article about car safety, a scientist who conducts experimental car crashes for the U.S. government can probably provide some valuable information. (But the testimony of the government car-crash expert will probably not be helpful if the author is writing about mysterious monsters unless the expert has some kind of valid experience with that topic as well.)

The key to evaluating testimonial evidence is determining whether the celebrity or expert is knowledgeable about the topic under consideration. The author must provide enough background so that the reader can judge whether the expert is qualified to provide valuable information.

In this article, Jorge Martin refers to the findings of "a qualified veterinary" to bolster his argument that the *chupacabras* is no ordinary animal. The expert's experience with animals should give him some credibility, although the reader must still try to assess the extent of this expert's knowledge.

Physical evidence (items 2, 4, and 12). Physical evidence can be used to prove or disprove a hypothesis. In police cases, physical evidence includes such things as fingerprints, DNA, and murder weapons. Most scientists prefer physical evidence over other kinds of evidence; the physical evidence can be examined directly, and with luck, it will provide definite answers. But even physical evidence can be controversial and can be interpreted in different ways. For example, in Martin's article he describes the bodies of the *chupacabras'* victims, their wounds, and the results of blood analyses. To the author, these are clear evidence that the *chupacabras* is not a known animal, but to some other people he mentions in the article—most notably government officials—the evidence can be explained in other ways.

A popular maxim that many scientists follow is called Occam's razor. Basically, it says that if there are two explanations that work, one simple or ordinary and one complex or bizarre, the simple one is more likely to be true. Some people think that Martin does not follow Occam's razor, and that he interprets evidence in a bizarre way when there are simpler answers (dogs or baboons, for instance) that fit the evidence just as well. What do you think—has Martin ignored simpler, more reasonable answers in favor of the bizarre?

Eyewitness testimony (items 6, 7, and 9). For some people, eyewitness accounts alone are enough to convince them that mysterious monsters are genuine. After all, history is filled with such sightings from credible people. But a scientist would examine such accounts very carefully because eyewitness testimony is notoriously unreliable.

Perhaps you know about the eyewitness experiment in which a group of people is sitting in a classroom listening to a lecture or doing some other activity. Suddenly, the classroom door bursts open, and a stranger enters. The stranger may "rob" one of the students or do something else dramatic. Then the stranger leaves.

A few moments later, the instructor asks the students to describe what they witnessed. Invariably, different students remember different things. One remembers that the stranger was of average height and weight; another remembers that he was thin or heavy. One remembers that he had red hair; another remembers that a hood covered the stranger's head. One remembers that he was carrying a weapon; another remembers that his hands were empty.

There are a lot of reasons for these different recollections. When something unexpected occurs, especially when it happens quickly or when it evinces great emotion, the mind is not prepared to remember details. Even when the event is expected, witnesses may remember things differently because they are not good observers. Or the witnesses may have preconceived ideas that influence their observations; for example, they may believe that robbers are male, so when they see a robber whose features are not clear, they assume the person must be male. Sometimes witnesses have recently experienced something that influences what they see; for instance, a person who has just come home from a scary movie and hears an unusual sound in the house may feel certain he or she is about to be set upon by a monster or a serial killer. In the case of the *chupacabras*, some critics point to Puerto Rico's history of vampire-type creatures and other traditions that might cause people from that country to leap to the conclusion that an unexpected animal death was caused by a mysterious monster.

For all these reasons and more, a reader has to be careful about accepting eyewitness testimony as the main source of evidence. In crime investigations, the police often try to find independent corroborating witnesses—several people who saw the same event and have not spoken with each other so that their accounts have not been influenced by anyone else's version. If two or more witnesses independently report the same details, the chances are better that the details are accurate. In this article, Martin does tell us that a woman named Madeline Tolentino and her neighbors *all* saw the creature walking down the street in broad daylight. Your job as a critical reader is to decide whether Martin's account of this incident is credible. Did he examine the situation carefully enough to conclude that the witnesses actually saw a *chupacabras*?

4. Consider Alternative Hypotheses

Once you have examined the types of evidence the author has provided and considered how valuable the evidence is in supporting the author's claims, review the article and decide whether the author has considered other possible explanations. If the author considers only one explanation for the evidence, he or she may be presenting a biased, or one-sided, view or may not have fully considered the issue. Does it seem to you that Jorge Martin has seriously considered any explanation for the strange goings-on in Puerto Rico besides a mysterious animal unlike any known on Earth?

5. Draw a Conclusion About the Author's Claim

After considering the evidence and alternative explanations, it is time to make a judgment, to decide whether the hypothesis makes sense. You can tally the evidence that does and does not support the hypothesis and see how many pros and cons you have. But that is really too simple. You will have to give more weight to some pieces of evidence than to others. What do you think is Martin's most convincing evidence? Is it strong enough to convince you that his hypothesis is true?

Exploring Further

Let's examine another article using hypothetical reasoning. Take a look at Joe Nickell's article, "'Mothman' Is a Barn Owl." Perhaps the first thing to notice is that Nickell comes to the Mothman topic with a bias against it. He is a prominent member of the skeptical organization the Committee for the Scientific Investigation of Claims of the Paranormal (CSICOP). He investigates many paranormal cases for CSICOP and writes regularly for the organization's magazine, *Skeptical Inquirer.* He is famous for debunking paranormal claims. A background like this could mean that an author will not treat a topic like Mothman fairly, but it does not *necessarily* mean that. When you know of such a potential bias, you must be sure to read carefully to see if the author seems to be writing objectively or if his or her background colors what he writes. What do you think—does Joe Nickell's treatment of the Mothman case seem to be objective or biased? Why do you think so?

Now let's review Nickell's article using the steps for hypothetical reasoning.

1. State a Hypothesis. In this case, the title of the article clearly states a hypothesis: What people call "Mothman" is really a common barn owl.

2. Gather the Author's Evidence. Here is some of Nickell's evidence:

1. Nickell says the descriptions of Mothman, which typically include large, glowing red eyes and a huge wingspan, "seem to fit the appearance of the common turkey vulture, which can have a six-foot wingspan and an unfeathered red head."

2. He cites Frank B. Gill's book *Ornithology*, which discusses how birds' eyes shine red in a light beam.

3. He gives a list of traits—including nocturnal habits; large, staring eyes that yield crimson eyeshine; long, powerful legs; noiseless, mothlike flight: and a tendency to hide in old buildings—and cites several bird authorities to show that these traits can be attributed to the common barn owl.

4. He notes that such things as darkness, surprise, and fear can "magnify" details for witnesses.

5. He calls the epidemic of Mothman sightings a "contagion."

6. He says we must choose between a "plausible, naturalistic explanation" (barn owl) and a "fanciful, incredible one" (a mysterious unknown monster) based on undependable eyewitness evidence.

3. Examine the Evidence. In his article, Nickell uses statements of opinion (item 1), statements of fact (item 3), and expert testimony (items 2 and 3). He also casts aspersions (items 5 and 6) and employs logical reasoning (items 1, 3, 4, and 6).

Statements of opinion (item 1). A statement of opinion cannot be proven true or false—it is simply what someone believes. (Statements of opinion often are based on or contain factual statements that can be verified. For example, "I think you are angry" is a statement of opinion, but it can be verified when your face turns red and you hit me in the nose.) In item 1, the opinion keywords are "seems to fit." The rest of the sentence provides verifiable information— the reader can look up information about turkey vultures to see if Nickell's opinion seems reasonable.

Whether we accept a statement of opinion as good supporting evidence depends on the nature of the opinion and what we think of the person giving it. For example, if our history teacher says, "Peace in the Middle East will not happen for a very long time," we may accept that as supporting evidence because we respect that teacher's knowledge about world events. But if the same teacher tells us, "Fashion models will be wearing white socks with their black trousers next year," we may be less inclined to take this opinion seriously unless he or she clearly keeps up with the latest fashion trends.

If an author relies heavily on opinion, you will have to decide if the author—or his or her sources—are reliable.

Statements of fact (item 3). Review the information on statements of fact. Does Nickell provide the sources of his facts so that the reader can verify them if desired? Do these facts provide good support for Nickell's thesis?

Expert testimony (items 2 and 3). Writers who are researchers, investigators, and scholars tend to cite a lot of experts who can help bolster their case. It is sometimes helpful to look up the original information to find out more about what the expert says about the topic. Some authors do not provide source information; they simply name the expert. But most serious researchers, investigators, and scholars provide full source information in footnotes or a text note so that the reader can find the original source, if desired. In this case, Nickell does provide detailed source information.

Casting aspersions (items 5 and 6). This practice belittles an opponent or opposing view to reduce its credibility. It sometimes includes name-calling or ridicule. Essentially, by showing contempt or dislike for the opponent or opposing view, the author hopes to influence the reader to feel that way, too.

In item 5, Nickell has called the Mothman sightings a "contagion." He uses the word to show how the sightings spread, much like a virulent sickness spreads, which is an unpleasant image. In item 6, he labels one point of view as "plausible" and the other as "fanciful" and "incredible." Which one is a reader more likely to believe is credible?

Many times, an author casts aspersions as a substitute for real evidence. You must read carefully to see if the author has provided evidence, too. You decide: Has Joe Nickell simply cast aspersions, or has he presented real evidence, too?

Logical reasoning (items 1, 3, 4, and 6). Review the information above about logical reasoning. Notice that items 1 and 3 of Nickell's evidence use the logic of Occam's razor: Nickell wants the reader to conclude that if what people saw has the characteristics of a turkey vulture or a barn owl, it is more likely to be one of these common birds than a bizarre, unknown monster.

4. *Consider Alternative Hypotheses.* Nickell does consider alternatives to his hypothesis that Mothman is a barn owl. He also notes that a single explanation (such as a barn owl) that will fit all encounters is unlikely. Do you think he has given enough consideration to alternative explanations for his hypothesis?

5. *Draw a Conclusion About the Author's Claim.* You decide: Does Joe Nickell make a good case for his hypothesis? What evidence most influences your decision?

Other Kinds of Evidence

Writers use many other kinds of evidence to support their hypotheses. The following are some common examples.

Anecdotal evidence. An anecdote is a brief story. Eyewitness testimony, described above, is one type of anecdotal evidence. A legend or traditional story that is related to the topic under discussion is another. Authors use anecdotes to illustrate a point or make an analogy.

Anecdotal evidence stands in contrast to hard evidence (including such things as facts, physical evidence, and statistical evidence), which investigators usually consider more significant than anecdotal evidence because it is easier to prove or disprove. However, anecdotal evidence can sometimes be strong and convincing, especially when multiple witnesses report the same thing.

Statistical or numerical evidence. When deciding whether something happened by chance or on purpose, statistical data can be important. For example, if a certain kind of monster evidence (such as unusual animal footprints) has appeared in the same vicinity again and again, the argument that a mysterious creature lives there is more credible. Authors also sometimes use numbers to show that a large number of people believe something or have experienced something. The authors hope the high numbers might convince some readers that a hypothesis is true. Evaluate all numerical claims carefully. Where did the numbers come from? If they are from a survey, how old is the survey? What do the numbers really mean?

Now You Do It!

Choose one article from this book that has not already been analyzed and use hypothetical reasoning to determine if the author's evidence supports the hypothesis. Here is a form you can use:

Name of article_____ Author_____

1. State the author's hypothesis.

2. List the evidence.

3. Examine the evidence. For each item you have listed under number 2, state what type of evidence it is (statement of fact, eyewitness testimony, etc.) and evaluate it: Does it appear to be valid evidence? Does it appear to support the author's hypothesis?

4. Consider alternative hypotheses. What alternative hypotheses does the author consider? Does he or she consider them fairly? If the author rejects them, does the rejection seem reasonable? Are there alternative explanations you believe should be considered? Explain.

5. Draw a conclusion about the hypothesis. Does the author adequately support his or her claim? Do you believe the author's hypothesis is credible? Explain.

For Further Research

General Sources

Books

Matthew Bille, *Rumors of Existence: Newly Discovered, Supposedly Extinct, and Unconfirmed Inhabitants of the Animal Kingdom*. Blaine, WA: Hancock House, 1995.

Jerome Clark, *Unexplained! Strange Sightings, Incredible Occurrences, and Puzzling Physical Phenomena*. Detroit: Visible Ink, 1999.

Jerome Clark and Loren Coleman, *Creatures of the Outer Edge*. New York: Warner Books, 1978.

Jerome Clark and Nancy Pear, *Strange and Unexplained Phenomena*. Detroit: Visible Ink, 1997.

Loren Coleman, *Mysterious America*. New York: Paraview, 2001.

Loren Coleman and Jerome Clark, *Cryptozoology A to Z*. New York: Simon and Schuster, 1999.

Kendrick Frazier, ed., *Science Confronts the Paranormal*. Amherst, NY: Prometheus Books, 1986.

Bernard Heuvelmans, *On the Track of Unknown Animals*. New York: Kegan Paul International, 1995.

John A. Keel, *The Complete Guide to Mysterious Beings*. Rev. ed. New York: Doubleday, 1994.

Roy Mackal, *Searching for Hidden Animals*. New York: Doubleday, 1980.

James F. McCloy and Ray Miller Jr., *Phantom of the Pines: More Tales of the Jersey Devil.* Moorestown, NJ: Middle Atlantic, 1998.

Joe Nickell, *Entities: Angels, Spirits, Demons, and Other Alien Beings.* Amherst, NY: Prometheus Books, 1995.

Karl P.N. Shuker, *From Flying Toads to Snakes with Wings.* St. Paul, MN: Llewellyn, 1997.

Gordon Stein, ed., *The Encyclopedia of the Paranormal.* Amherst, NY: Prometheus Books, 1996.

Samantha Weinberg, *Fish Caught in Time: The Search for the Coelacanth.* New York: HarperPerennial, 2000.

Colin Wilson with Damon Wilson, *The Encyclopedia of Unsolved Mysteries.* Chicago: Contemporary Books, 1988.

Websites

Anomalies, http://anomalyinfo.com. This site describes itself as "a database of paranormal (and allegedly paranormal) events, objects, and people, compiled from a variety of sources."

Committee for the Scientific Investigation of Claims of the Paranormal (CSICOP), www.csicop.org. The most prominent skeptical organization in the United States, CSICOP encourages critical thinking and skepticism about paranormal and other "fringe" topics.

Creature Chronicles, http://home.fuse.net/rschaffner. Operated by Ron Schaffner, a cryptozoology enthusiast, the site offers, among other things, archived newspaper articles, research files, and a strong list of links.

Cryptozoology, www.pibburns.com/cryptozo.htm. Operated by cryptozoology enthusiast Pib Burns, this site offers one of the most extensive lists of links related to this topic.

Pseudoscience, Paranormal, Skepticism, http://suhep.phy.syr.edu/courses/modules/PSEUDO/pseudo.html. Articles present skeptical views of mysterious monsters and other paranormal topics.

The Skeptic's Dictionary, www.skepdic.com. Operated by Robert T. Carroll, this site presents a skeptical view of more than four hundred "strange beliefs, amusing deceptions, and dangerous delusions," including ghosts and hauntings.

Unexplained Mysteries, www.unexplained-mysteries.com. This site provides current news and archived articles covering the gamut of paranormal subject matter.

The UnMuseum: Science over the Edge, www.unmuseum. org/soearch/over0501.htm. This website contains news stories related to cryptozoology and other "edge-of-science" topics.

Sources About the Mysterious Monsters Covered in This Book

Mothman

Loren Coleman, *Mothman and Other Curious Encounters.* New York: Paraview, 2002.

———, *The Mothman Prophecies.* New York: Saturday Review, 1975.

Dennie Sargent Jr. and Jeff Wamsley, *Mothman: The Facts Behind the Legend.* Point Pleasant, WV: Mothman Lives, 2002.

Chupacabras

David Adams, "The Weird Tale of the Goatsucker," *St. Petersburg Times,* March 21, 1996. http://web.archive.org/web/19970723160055/www.princeton.edu/~accion/chupa19. html.

The Chupacabra Homepage, http://web.archive.org/web/19970719040917/http://www.princeton.edu/~accion/

chupa.html. Archived pages of a now-defunct website devoted to the *chupacabras.*

Scott Corrales, *Chupacabras and Other Mysteries.* Murfreesboro, TN: Greenleaf, 1997.

Robert Sheaffer, "The Great Chupacabra Conspiracy," *Skeptical Inquirer,* March/April 2001, pp. 19–21.

Giant Birds

Mark Chorvinsky, "Cowboys and Dragons: Unraveling the Mystery of the Thunderbird Photograph," Parts 1 and 2, *StrangeMagazine.* www.strangemag.com.

Loren Coleman, "Mysterious World," *Fate,* January 2001.

Mark Hall, *Thunderbirds! The Living Legend of Giant Birds.* Bloomington, MN: Mark A. Hall Publications and Research, 1998.

Index

Creatures of the Outer Edge
(Coleman and Clark), 73
Crichton, Michael, 103, 104
Cryptology Review (journal), 12
cryptozoology, 8, 10–12, 16

Diaz-Bolio, José, 64, 65, 111
dinosaurs. *See* pterodactyls
disinformation programs,
56–57
see also cover-ups
Disneyland of the Gods (Keel),
26
Dover Demon
eyewitness reports of,
74–78
as moose, 114–19
UFO research and, 78
Dowd, Alison, 43
Doyle, Arthur Conan,
103–105
dragons, 59, 61
see also chupacabras;
pterodactyls

evidence
animal deaths as, 37,
38–41, 44, 49–50, 66
eyewitness reports as, 85–86
Occam's razor theory and,
12
photographs as, 39, 40–41,
44, 49–50, 65–66,
102–109
shortcomings of, 10–11, 12,
85–86
tracks as, 37
see also specific names of
monsters
"eyeburn," 31

Fate (magazine), 65
feathered serpent, 64–65

flying reptiles. *See* pterodactyls
Fogg, Ed, 78
Fortean Times (magazine), 107,
108
fossil fish, 8–9
fossils, 8–9, 60, 62
Friedman, Robert, 97

Garcia, Hector, 49
genetic experimentation, 44,
54–55, 56
giant bird, 13
see also pterodactyls
Gill, Frank B., 84
goatsucker. *See chupacabras*
government agents, 26
see also "Men in Black"
Greeley, Andrew, 15
Greenwell, Richard, 111
Grinker, Richard, 99

Hall, Mark, 107
Harrison, J., 111–12
Heuvelmans, Bernard, 8, 10
"high strangeness," 26

Jurassic Park (film), 103

Kanchen, Tsian, 54–55
Keel, John A.
biographical information
about, 25
on fascination with
monsters, 13–14
Mothman writings of, 19,
83
paranormal theories of, 26
photograph of alleged
pterodactyl and, 65
Kottmeyer, Martin S., 114

Listening Post (Olson), 80
Loch Ness monster, 10